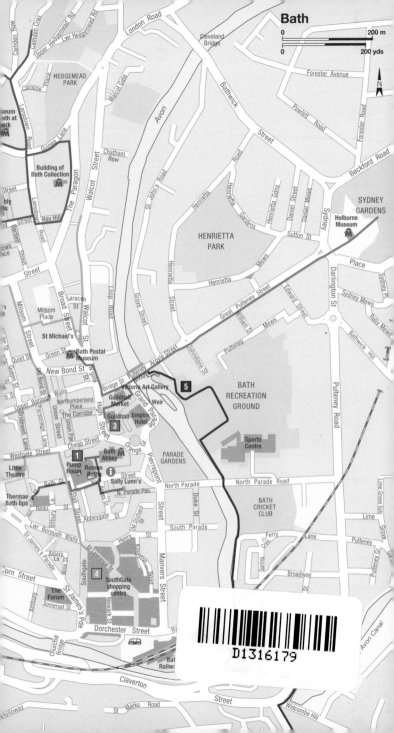

INSIGHT GUIDES

Great Breaks

BATH

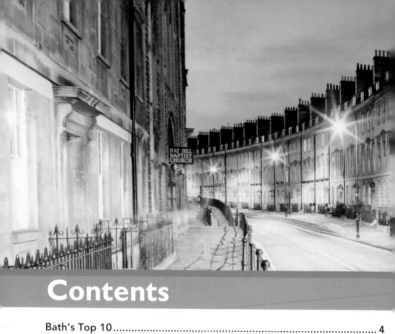

Contents

Bath's Top 10

Magnificent Georgian architecture, historic attractions, modern spa facilities, and a host of cultural festivals... here at a glance is why Bath is one of the few cities to have achieved Unesco World Heritage Site status

▲ **Roman Baths** *(p.15)*. The city's most popular tourist attraction, the baths are a vivid reminder of exactly what the Romans did for us.

▲ **Thermae Bath Spa** *(p.23)*. Bath's thermal springs are its *raison d'être*, and this modern facility allows you to be pampered in style while you take the waters.

▲ **The Royal Crescent and the Circus** *(p.29)*. The most picturesque terraces in the country, these Georgian gems are 18th-century architecture at its best.

▶ **Bath Abbey** *(p.19)*. The heart of the city in the Middle Ages, the site of the magnificent Abbey is where Edgar, England's first king, was crowned.

▲ **Assembly Rooms** *(p.32)*. No Jane Austen adaptation is complete without a scene set in these rooms that were at the centre of Georgian society. The building also houses the impressive Fashion Museum.

▼ **Prior Park** *(p.65)*. The original show home, this was built by 18th-century businessman Ralph Allen to demonstrate the beauty of the honey-coloured stone that now dominates the city.

▼ **Pump Room** *(p.18)*. Experience a taste of Georgian social life in this elegant room where you can also sample the spa water (if you're brave enough).

▲ **Festivals** *(p.10)*. The city's annual calendar of festivals offers something for everyone, from comedy to films and literature to jazz.

▼ **Milsom Street** *(p.55)*. Voted the country's favourite street for fashion, and just a small part of a city renowned for its diverse range of independent shops.

▲ **Pulteney Bridge** *(p.47)*. A beautiful bridge-cum-shopping arcade overlooking the River Avon.

A Georgian Jewel

With its beautiful, honey-coloured stone and exquisite architecture, Bath makes a striking first impression, attracting several million visitors each year

Declared a Unesco World Heritage Site in 1987, Bath has been attracting visitors since pre-Roman times, drawn to its natural spring waters. Today it is a gracious and beautiful city in an incomparable setting, and most visitors find themselves falling in love with it. All significant stages of English history are represented here, from the Roman Baths to medieval Bath Abbey, from the Georgian splendour of the Royal Crescent to the modern Thermae Bath Spa development – the only place in Britain where you can bathe in natural hot spring water. Thanks to its rich past and architectural heritage, combined with a vibrant shopping centre, year-round festivals and lively entertainment scene, Bath is one of Britain's most appealing cities.

LANDSCAPE AND CLIMATE

The city lies cradled amid several hills in the Mendips, home to its famous pale stone as well as the hot springs that have been the source of its popu-

larity since Celtic times. Dissected by the Avon River, which flows into the Severn estuary at Avonmouth, the Kennet and Avon Canal (1810) and the Great Western Railway (1841), the city covers 11 hilly sq miles (29 sq km). It centres on the ancient Abbey and Roman Baths, with Georgian Bath spreading north to the Upper Town and east over the river to Bathwick.

It is situated 97 miles (156km) west of London and 13 miles (21km) southeast of the large port city of Bristol. Bath has a population of 90,000, though this number is boosted by almost four million tourists a year and out-of-towners who come for its shops, restaurants, theatre and concerts. The surrounding hills give Bath its steep streets and make its buildings appear to climb the slopes. While in many minds the city is associated with middle-class retirees, its population is a mix of old and young, the latter boosted by a strong student presence from Bath University, Bath Spa University, and City of Bath College.

Above: view of Bath Abbey and the Pump Room. **Below**: intricate fan vaulting inside Bath Abbey.

Above: the Roman Baths complex offers a fascinating insight into the beliefs and customs of Ancient Rome.

Bath, like the rest of southwest England, has a temperate climate and is generally wetter and milder than much of the rest of England. January is the coldest month with mean minimum temperatures between 1° and 2°C (34–36°F), while July and August are generally the warmest months, with a mean daily maximum of around 21°C (70°F). When the sun shines in Bath, its buildings seem to come truly alive, and there are plenty of open spaces and parks to enjoy.

A RICH HISTORY

In the 1st century AD, the Romans built a temple and baths on the site of the sacred hot springs, which attracted pilgrims from all over the Roman Empire who would come to petition the god Sulis Minerva and to bathe in the healing waters. When the Romans abandoned Britain in the 5th century AD, Bath fell into relative decline.

The city was revived in the 18th century during a period known as the Georgian era, referring to the reign of four kings named George, from 1714–1830. During this time, a long-neglected provincial retreat was transformed into a fashionable spa with the help of three self-made men: Richard (Beau) Nash, a charismatic dandy, Ralph Allen, an astute businessman, and John Wood, a trail-blazing architect. Developments in the social sphere, led by Master of Ceremonies Nash (also known unofficially as the King of Bath), were accompanied by the planning and building of what amounted to a new city, in which Allen and Wood played significant roles. Allen made his fortune by transforming and modernising the postal system, making him one of the founders of the modern post office. Having acquired the nearby quarries of

Above: statue of the celebrated dandy Beau Nash in the Pump Room.

ⒺFood and Drink

Bath boasts a number of local spe-
cialites worth sampling. Sally Lunn
buns have long been baked in Bath
and are still available at the restaurant of the same name. The famous
Bath Soft Cheese is a reproduction
of a lost recipe dating back to the
time of Admiral Lord Nelson, while
Wyfe of Bath cheese is quickly
catching up in terms of popularity
and reputation. The Bath Oliver is
a dry-baked biscuit invented in the
18th century by Dr William Oliver,
an early anti-obesity campaigner.

Above: Sally Lunn's – the perfect
place for afternoon tea.

local stone, he encouraged the brilliant
young architect, John Wood the elder,
to realise his visions in Bath stone. The
legacy of Wood and his son can be
seen in the shape of the Royal Crescent, the Circus, Queen Square, the
Assembly Rooms and Prior Park, with
other architects following their lead to
create a bustling, elegant Georgian city
that still thrives today.

All the traditions of Bath from
that era – the healing of the sick, the
cultivation of the arts and the entertainment of visitors – were carried
on into the 19th and 20th centuries
and are still evident today. With its
Thermae Bath Spa complex, which
has attracted about 200,000 visitors
annually since opening in 2006, the
city has returned to its roots, allowing
visitors a unique opportunity in Britain
to enjoy the natural thermal waters
in a striking contemporary setting,
alongside up-to-the-minute health and
beauty treatments. The development
was voted the best spa in the world
for the second time at the Ultra Travel
awards in 2010.

The city used to have an important
manufacturing sector, including the
famed crane makers Stothert & Pitt,
but manufacturing is now in decline
in the city, which looks instead to
its growing technology, creative and
service-oriented industries, alongside
its crucial tourism sector.

Find our recommended restaurants
at the end of each Tour. Below is a Price
Guide to help you make your choice.

Eating Out Price Guide

Two-course meal for one person,
including a glass of wine.

£££	over £30
£££	over £30
££	£15–30
£	under £15

Guide to Coloured Boxes

ⒺEating	This guide is dotted with coloured boxes providing additional practical and cultural infor- mation to make the most of your visit. Here is a guide to the coding system.
ⒻFact	
ⒼGreen	
ⓀKids	
ⓈShopping	
ⓋView	

Festivals in Bath

Rather than concentrating on one large festival, Bath has a year-round series of cultural events, with regular highlights on the calendar including the Bath International Music Festival, which coincides with a lively Fringe, and other events covering literature, children's books, Mozart, Jane Austen, comedy, cinema, fashion and food and drink.

BATH INTERNATIONAL MUSIC FESTIVAL

The largest of the Bath festivals has an illustrious artistic history and has long been a well-established event of national significance and international reputation, presenting a dynamic mix of world-class performers. The festival showcases a range of high-quality events featuring orchestral and classical virtuosos, jazz giants, folk, roots and world musicians, innovative collaborations and unique commissions. Performers and events at the festival have included the English National Ballet, the London Symphony Orchestra, conductor Sir Colin Davis, pop and folk singer Eddi Reader, jazz and soul legend Booker T, Motown diva Martha Reeves, and a spectacular production of Handel's *Israel in Egypt* at the Roman Baths.

BATH FRINGE FESTIVAL

Since 1981, the Fringe has provided a platform for alternative forms of entertainment. The festival is among the oldest continually operating in England, and includes around 200 events, taking place around the late May Bank Holiday. Past performers include comedians Bill Bailey, Lee Evans, Arthur Smith (whose hit West End play *An Evening with Gary Lineker* made its debut in Bath), Jeremy Hardy, Julian Clary, Rich Hall and John Hegley, and musicians Beth Rowley, Peter Hammill and Jah Wobble.

LITERATURE FESTIVALS

Launched in 1995, the Bath Literature Festival offers stimulating debate, lively conversations and a chance to meet authors. The festival has special events pairing like-minded authors, debates on topical issues, and specially commissioned work by leading contemporary writers. Each festival features the Bath Big Read, when the city is invited to read a new novel and discuss it with the author. Recent guests have included Man Booker Prize winner Hilary Mantel, poet laureate Carol Ann Duffy, and celebrated *Harry Potter* author JK Rowling.

The Children's Literature Festival, launched in 2007, has already become a popular and established part of the

Above: the Bath Fringe Festival attracts all sorts of performers.

Above: the annual Jane Austen Festival features a costumed parade.

festival's calendar, drawing the biggest names in children's writing, including Michael Morpurgo, Jacqueline Wilson and Anthony Horowitz, as well as attracting stars such as Harry Hill. More fun than its senior counterpart, the festival has proved a big hit with youngsters and adults alike and is the UK's largest dedicated festival celebrating children's books.

FROM JANE AUSTEN TO MOZART

Each year the life and work of Jane Austen are celebrated with a series of events, including Europe's largest Regency costumed parade. There are also concerts, talks, music events and dance. Mozart's link to Bath is less clear, but, since 1990, the festival celebrates the maestro's music, and that of his contemporaries or those influenced by him, in a nine-day feast of classical music.

Established in 1991, the Bath Film Festival shows premieres and films that would not normally make it to the city, as well as having outdoor screenings and offering a chance to meet film-makers including local directors and producers such as Ken Loach and Stephen Woolley.

Bath in Fashion marks the city's status as an epicentre of style. The city becomes a huge catwalk featuring shows, workshops, films and exhibitions from fashion's biggest names. Previous guests include shoe designer and Bath resident Manolo Blahnik.

More recent arrivals on the scene include the Bath Comedy Festival, which starts, appropriately, on April Fool's Day, and the Great Bath Feast, launched in 2012. Celebrating fantastic food and drink from in and around the city, on the menu are demonstrations from top chefs, hands-on cookery classes and opportunities to sample plenty of Bath's tastiest produce.

F Festivals

Bath International Music Festival Runs for 12 days in late May/early June. www.bathmusicfest.org.uk

Bath Fringe Festival Runs for 17 days in late May/early June. www.bathfringe.co.uk

Bath Literature Festival Runs over 10 days in late February/early March. www.bathlitfest.org.uk

Bath Children's Literature Festival Runs for 10 days in late September/early October. www.bathfestivals.org.uk/childrens-literature

Jane Austen Festival Runs over nine days in mid-September. www.janeausten.co.uk/festivalhome

Bath Mozart Festival Runs for nine days in November. www.bathmozartfest.org.uk

Bath Film Festival Runs for 11 days in mid-November. www.bathfilmfestival.org.uk

Bath in Fashion Runs for a week in mid-April. www.bathinfashion.co.uk

Bath Comedy Festival Runs for 10 days in late March/early April. www.bathcomedyfestival.co.uk

The Great Bath Feast Runs over a period of one month in September or October. www.greatbathfeast.co.uk

Tour 1

The Ancient Centre and a Modern Spa

This walk in the heart of the city is about a third of a mile (0.5km) long and can be done in less than an hour, but you could happily spend a full day taking in all the highlights

This tour takes you through Bath's 2,000-year history from the Roman Baths, via the Medieval Abbey and the Pump Room, to a modern spa complex, where you can swim in the natural thermal waters.

Bath's most popular visitor attraction, and finalist in the VisitEngland Awards for Excellence 2013, the Roman Baths is the ideal place to start both geographically and historically, as this is where the Bath we know today began. The Romans invaded Britain in AD43 and, after discovering the healing waters, they developed a city called Aquae Sulis, which included a bathing complex and temple. The surviving parts of that 2,000-year-old structure

can be viewed alongside recreations of what it was like to be a Roman in Bath two millennia ago. Most of the complex is Victorian but much work has been done recently to improve the facilities, with modern techniques used to bring the past to life. You should set aside at least two hours to get the most out of your visit.

Preceding pages: one of several lions dotted around the city. **Left**: the Roman Baths and the Abbey Courtyard. **Above**: Gorgon's Head.

ROMAN BATHS

The main entrance to the **Roman Baths** ❶ (tel: 01225 477785; www. romanbaths.co.uk; daily Mar–June and Sept–Oct 9am–6pm, July–Aug 9am–10pm, Nov–Feb 9.30am–5.30pm, last entry 1 hour before closing; charge) is in Abbey Church Yard. The baths themselves are below the modern street level and the site also features a Sacred Spring, a Roman Temple, a

Roman Bath House and a museum with finds from the Roman Baths. The buildings above street level date from the 19th century.

You begin your visit in the Victorian reception hall, where you can buy a ticket and pick up a personal audioguide at no extra cost. These informative guides are available in eight languages, English, French, German, Italian, Japanese, Mandarin, Spanish and Russian. There are also separate commentaries aimed at children, featuring Roman characters and their stories, and some of the highlights are described by the writer Bill Bryson in his usual witty and incisive way. In the entrance, formerly a concert hall, the impressive ceiling is decorated with images of the four seasons and surmounted by an elegant dome.

As you walk through to the terrace, you get your first glimpse from above of the magnificent Great Bath, lined with statues of Roman emperors and other leaders. Bryson rightly describes the view from one corner of the terrace, taking in Bath Abbey in the background, as one of the finest in the country. When ready, follow the self-guided tour that leads to ground level.

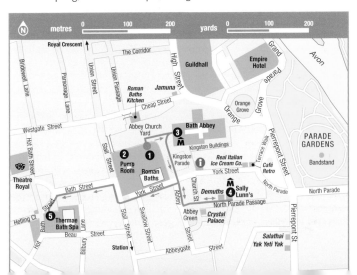

Above: the Great Bath looks particularly special at night when it's lit by torches.

Sacred Spring

You next pass the King's Bath, site of the Sacred Spring. Hot water at a temperature of 114°F (46°C) rises here at a rate of 240,000 gallons (1,170,000 litres) per day as it has been doing for thousands of years. In the past this natural phenomenon was beyond human understanding and was believed to be the work of the ancient gods. In Roman times a great Temple was built next to the spring dedicated to the goddess Sulis Minerva, a deity with healing powers. The mineral-rich water from the Sacred Spring supplied a magnificent bathhouse that attracted visitors from across the Roman Empire. Many of these visitors would have thrown objects into the Sacred Spring as offerings to the goddess, including more than 12,000 Roman coins. Curses, inscribed on pewter or lead sheets, also abound, some written backwards. These generally solicit help or revenge for mundane grievances, such as the theft of a glove or napkin ring.

The Temple

You next encounter one of only two truly classical temples known from Ro-

man Britain and the place where the cult statue of the goddess Sulis Minerva was housed. The great ornamental pediment survives and has been re-erected in the Roman Baths Museum. Its centrepiece is the image of a fearsome head carved in Bath stone, thought to be the Gorgon's Head, a powerful symbol of Sulis Minerva.

The temple courtyard houses the stunning gilded bronze head of Minerva, one of the best-known objects from Roman Britain and one of the museum's highlights. The bronze, minus helmet (you can see the rivet holes where this would have been held in place), was discovered in 1727 by workmen in nearby Stall Street and was the first intimation of the marvellous Roman ruins below Georgian Bath. The head is probably from a statue of the deity, which would have stood within her Temple beside the Sacred Spring.

The Roman Baths houses a museum collection of outstanding quality and international significance. Many of the objects in the museum tell us about the people who lived and worked in the area and those who visited the spa and temple. This area includes film projections of Roman characters to give visitors a sense of how the Romans lived and worshipped.

Before moving on to the Great Bath, you get a glimpse of the Roman plumbing and drainage system, which is still largely in place and shows the ingenuity of the Roman engineers. Lead pipes were used to carry hot spa water around the site using gravity flow. The Spring overflow is where surplus water from the Spring flows out to a Roman drain, which carries all the spa water from the site to the River Avon 1,300ft (400m) away.

The Great Bath

This is the highlight of the tour and the best place to see the water at close quarters. Laden with 43 different minerals, including iron, which stains the stone red, the water is thought to spring from 2 miles (3km) beneath the Mendip Hills, on which it fell as rain up to 10,000 years ago. Its green colour is caused by light reacting with algae: when the baths were roofed over, as they were in Roman times, the water would have been clear (a section of the vaulted roof is propped up against the wall at the west end of the Great Bath). The water is continually renewed.

Though much of the site is a Victorian re-creation, you still get a great feel for how extraordinary the complex would have been in Roman times, with its amazing vaulted roof. There are impressive models in the museum section that show the scale and grandeur of the development, revealing exactly what the Romans did for us in Bath. If you're visiting in July and August, make sure you see the Great Bath in the evening, when the area is lit by torches. There are costumed characters around the Great Bath to fill you in on the history and to give an idea of the sort of people who used the site.

The Great Bath was essentially a swimming bath, with alcoves for beauty treatments and entertainment (much like the new Thermae Bath Spa development, see p.23). The East Baths were for serious ablutions, offering a tepidarium (warm room), where oils were applied and massages

Below: the gilded bronze head of the goddess Sulis Minerva.

given, and a caldarium (hot room) with steam hypocaust flooring which would have provided heating.

In the West baths, the Circular Bath was a cold plunge pool whose waters were piped in specially. Also here is the King's Bath, which is overlooked by the Pump Room. In a niche on one side of the bath is a statue of King Bladud, the city's mythical founder (see p.59).

THE PUMP ROOM

You exit the museum through a shop, but if you don't fancy picking up a gift with a Roman or Georgian flavour, you can exit via the **Pump Room** ❷ (tel: 01225 444477; www.roman baths.co.uk; daily 9.30am–5pm), one of the social hubs of Bath since the Georgian era. Here you can sample the spa water if you're brave enough (it's free if you have a Roman Baths ticket, small charge otherwise). It's an acquired taste and leaves you with sympathy for the Georgians who were encouraged to drink as much as a gallon (4.5 litres) a day. The spa water is dispensed from a decorative 19th-century drinking fountain.

Admission to the Pump Room is free, so you can walk along the sides and gaze at the splendour of the striking neoclassical salon. If you have time (and you may have to queue when it's busy), you can have morning coffee, lunch or afternoon tea in an elegant setting, listening to the soothing sounds of a pianist or the Pump Room trio – the longest-established resident ensemble in Europe – while imagining what this stunning scene would have been like in Jane Austen's time.

The Pump Room, built between 1790 and 1795, is a sumptuous building with its great columns, curved recesses and musicians' gallery. It was here that the therapeutic waters, pumped directly from the source, could be sampled in comfort. As the doctors of the day recommended taking the waters before breakfast, the Pump Room was open from 6am onwards. It was also a social forum complete with musical entertainment, though not filled with tables and chairs as it is today. In the 1800s, the custom was to walk about the room to see and be seen.

Below: in Georgian times, visitors would come to the Pump Room before breakfast to take the waters and mingle.

Above: the hot spa water dispensed in the Pump Room was once believed to cure all manner of ailments.

BATH ABBEY

So far, we've covered Roman times and the Georgian era, but now it's time to step into the Middle Ages with the awesome abbey, the third to be built on this site. The first abbey was where Edgar, the first king of all England, was crowned in 973. Edgar introduced the Benedictine monks who were to control the abbey, and thus the growing medieval town, for the next 500 years.

Bath Abbey ❸ (www.bathabbey. org; daily 9am–6pm, with exceptions during services; suggested charge), the heart of Bath in the Middle Ages, is a short walk from the entrance of the Roman Baths across Abbey Church Yard.

In 1107, in the wake of the Norman conquest, the Bishop of Somerset moved the seat of the bishopric from Wells to Bath (a controversial move that eventually led to the pope renaming the diocese Bath and Wells) and built a Norman church on the site of the Saxon one. This lasted until 1499, when Bishop Oliver King, inspired by a dream, rebuilt the church in the late English Gothic style characterised by flying buttresses, wide windows and fan vaulting. It remains one of the few great Medieval churches to have been built to its original design, without the distractions of later additions or alterations.

The Dissolution of the Monasteries by Henry VIII in 1539 brought the work to a halt, leaving the nave without a roof. Its eventual completion is said to have come about nearly a century later after James Montague, Bishop of Bath and Wells, sought shelter here while walking in a storm with Sir John Harrington, a godson of Queen Elizabeth I. According to the story, the rain-soaked Harrington turned to Montague and

Ⓚ Abbey Church Yard Buskers

The space in front of the Abbey and the Roman Baths is a favourite spot for the city's buskers, some of whom provide excellent entertainment that will keep children amused for hours. The daily rota for these hour-long pitches is decided at a buskers' meeting at 10am each day. On a summer evening the Bizarre Bath comedy tour show up at around 9pm – it's customary for the buskers to stop playing until they have finished.

Above: the Abbey's imposing West Front overlooks Abbey Church Yard.

Above: the area around the Abbey is often home to interesting art exhibits.

said, 'If the church does not keep us safe from the water above, how shall it save others from the fires below?', prompting the bishop to commission a roof, which was completed after a nationwide appeal for funds backed by Queen Elizabeth I.

The West Front and Interior

The Abbey describes itself as the place where earth and heaven meet. The entrance to the abbey is through the West Front, with its Jacob's Ladder, which symbolically depicts Bishop King's dream of ladders reaching to heaven with falling and rising angels. The porous Bath stone had meant that some of the figures were becoming badly worn, but after the West Front was cleaned in the 1990s, it has been restored to its former glory. Take a look at the statues in the alcoves either side of the main wooden door. Saint Peter on the left is shorter and with a far less striking beard than St Paul. It turns out Peter's head was reputedly decapitated by Cromwell's men during the English Civil War and was subsequently rebuilt using the stone from his once magnificent beard.

Inside, the vast windows fill the abbey with light, earning it the epithet Lantern of the West during Elizabethan times. The overall impression inside is of light and height. The east window depicts 56 scenes in the Life of Christ in brilliant stained glass. The stained glass was damaged by World

Above: Bishop of Bath and Wells from 1608–18, James Montague's coat of arms can be seen on the west door.

War II bombs and was restored by a direct descendant of the man who created the original glass.

Overhead stretches the breathtakingly beautiful fan vaulting. This was added in two stages: the first (over the chancel) by William Vertue, master mason to Henry VII, when the abbey was built, and the rest in the mid-19th century during restorations by George Gilbert Scott. At that time, houses had been allowed to crowd up against the Abbey. On the north side, you can still see the marks left by the subsequently demolished houses.

Among the delights of the abbey are the memorials to famous city residents and guests who died in Bath (it is estimated that 3,879 bodies lie beneath the stone floors). There are more wall plaques marking the dead here than anywhere else in Britain other than Westminster Abbey. Many give a vivid, sometimes tantalising, glimpse of their subject's life, including the one to James Bassett, who 'in the Moment of Social Pleasure, received a fall, which soon deprived him of life.'

Don't miss the one dedicated to Beau Nash ('Ricardi Nash', 'Elegantiae Arbiter'). The former Master of Ceremonies, who helped transform the

Above: the walls of the Abbey are lined with memorial plaques.

city's fortunes in the 1700s, died at the age of 86, impoverished and enfeebled. Nonetheless, his former brilliance was recalled at his death and the corporation funded a splendid funeral. Other well-known names include Sir Isaac Pitman, the inventor of shorthand, whose memorial is adorned with a winged pen, and the actor James Quin, whose epitaph was written by his friend and fellow thespian David Garrick.

You can also take a tour of the Abbey's Tower (charge). The guided

Ⓢ Bath Christmas Market

The popular German-style Christmas market (www.bathchristmasmarket. co.uk), which takes over the area around the Abbey from late November until mid-December, is one of the highlights of the festive season. Over 100 wooden chalets offer a wide variety of unusual gifts and tempting treats, drawing in tourists from all over Britain and abroad. It's a perfect place to find a festive gift or to simply soak up the atmosphere.

Above: grab a cup of mulled wine and browse the Christmas Market.

Real Italian Ice Cream

If the kids are flagging, the best way to revive them is with a yummy ice cream. The Real Italian Ice Cream Co at 17 York Street serves delicious *gelati*, just like the ones you get in Italy. There is a great choice of flavours, including some rarities, which vary with the season. Also serves coffee and crêpes.

tour takes 45–50 minutes and includes standing on top of the Abbey's vaulted ceiling, sitting behind the clock face, seeing the Abbey bells and a bird's-eye view of Bath. There are 212 steps to the top of the Tower arranged in two spiral staircases.

The Abbey is still an active Christian church and works hard to remain part of the community, hosting carol concerts and other musical events alongside its church services. It has also acted as a venue for film screenings and for exhibitions, while revellers gather in Abbey Church Yard to see in the new year.

SALLY LUNN'S

From the Abbey it is a short hop to this picture-postcard restaurant-cum-museum. Head south from the Abbey, keeping the Roman Baths on your right and the Tourist Information Centre on your left, cross York Street into Abbey Street and turn left as you enter Abbey Green into North Parade Passage – the huge plane tree standing before you was planted about 1790. **Sally Lunn's** ❹ (4 North Parade Passage; tel: 01225 461634; www. sallylunns.co.uk; Mon–Sat 10am–9.30pm, Sun 11am–9pm) claims to be the oldest surviving house in Bath (c.1482, with a 17th-century facade prettified by window boxes and olde-worlde signs). This is a rare example in Bath of an early Stuart house. Sally Lunn was said to be a French refugee who arrived in England more than 300 years ago. The restaurant is famous for a special kind of bun *(see p.9)*, which has been made on the premises since the 1680s. This bun, still baked to a secret recipe, became a popular treat in Georgian England as its taste and lightness meant it could

Below: the intricate fan vaulting inside Bath Abbey was added by the Victorians in 1860 when the original roof of 1608 was replaced.

Above: cream tea at Sally Lunn's.

be enjoyed with sweet or savoury accompaniments. The basement museum contains a 17th-century oven and archaeological finds excavated on the site.

THERMAE BATH SPA

From Sally Lunn's, head west back to Abbey Street, go north to York Street, turn left, passing under an impressive

Above: Sally Lunn's house is one of the oldest buildings in Bath.

arch that was actually built to disguise some of the pipework to the Roman Baths, and turn right at Stall Street and then left on Bath Street, at the end of which is Bath's most exciting modern development, the **Thermae Bath Spa ❺** (6–8 Hot Bath Street; tel: 0844 888 0844 or 01225 331234; www.thermaebathspa.com; daily 9am– 9.30pm, last entry 7pm; charge). It was built to allow visitors the chance to bathe once again in the city's spring waters as people have been doing since Roman times. Up until the 1970s, visitors were still occasionally able to swim in the Roman Baths, but the local authorities banned bathing in 1978 amid safety concerns over the threat of infectious diseases. Despite a formal opening in 2003 with a spectacular concert headed by the Three Tenors (the late Luciano Pavarotti, Plácido Domingo and Jose Carreras), the project ran seriously behind schedule and over budget as a result of legal disputes with contractors. Budgeted costs spiralled from an estimated £13 million to £45 million, and it eventually opened its doors in 2006.

Modern architecture

The main spa has two natural thermal baths, a rooftop pool and an in-

> **F Mayor of Bath Guides**
>
> The Mayor of Bath's honorary guides have been showing visitors around the city since 1934. The free two-hour walking tours begin at the Roman Baths and provide a snapshot of the city's history and important buildings. The volunteer guides, who do not accept tips, turn out in all weathers (tel: 01225 477411; www.bathguides.org.uk; Sun–Fri 10.30am and 2pm, Sat 10.30am, May–Sept Tue, and Thur 7pm).

Above: the Thermae Spa's striking glass and Bath-stone exterior.

door one, a large steam room glass-partitioned into four circular zones, and body treatment facilities. Most of the facilities are in a modern building designed by Grimshaw Architects, with the older Cross Bath (10am–8pm, last entry 6pm) in a separate building.

Nicholas Grimshaw's design, strikingly contemporary in a city renowned for its conservatism, is made up of a giant stone cube enveloped by glass, with curves and sinuous lines inside.

Two-hour, four-hour and all-day mixed-sex sessions (bathing costumes must be worn; no children under 16; children over 12 are allowed in the

Below: the idyllic open-air pool on top of the Thermae baths.

Cross Bath if accompanied by an adult) are available without booking, though treatments (including hydrotherapy, body wraps, mud treatments, facials, flotation therapy and massage) must be booked.

Inside the spa

As you can't book for the spa sessions, you may face queues at busy times (such as weekend mornings). Towels, robes and slippers are not included in the entrance fee but can be hired. You can save money by bringing your own towel or borrowing one from your hotel if you're staying in the city. A Smart-Band, provided on your arrival, acts as the key for your locker and is valid for the length of your session (you are allowed an extra 15 minutes for showering etc but will be charged extra if you exceed your time limit).

The spa's crowning glory is its open-air rooftop pool. Submerged in the hot mineral waters, you can take in beautiful views of the Abbey and the surrounding countryside, and it is particularly evocative at twilight and after dark. Head down to the steam rooms, each one gently infused with an essential oil

Above: sea-horse mosaic in the Roman Baths (4th century AD).

such as mountain pine, eucalyptus mint, jasmine or lavender. A central waterfall shower helps you to cool off. On the ground floor is the Minerva Bath, an indoor pool that is the largest of the thermal baths. Round off your visit with another trip to the open-air pool. The complex also has a restaurant (10am–8.15pm). The Good Spa Guide describes the development as 'a real people's spa', while one visitor said the experience was 'like swimming in silk'.

◨ Eating Out

Café Retro
18 York Street; tel: 01225 339347; www.caferetro.co.uk; Mon–Fri 9am–4pm, Sat 9am–5pm, Sun 10am–5pm.
A relaxed café offering good-value all-day breakfasts, salads, sandwiches, panini and burgers. £

Crystal Palace
10–11 Abbey Green; tel: 01225 482666; www.crystalpalacepub.co.uk; Mon–Sat 11am–11pm, Sun noon–10.30pm.
Pub serving cask ales and traditional fare, such as its signature fish and chips and sausages and mash, alongside more interesting sharing platters, which can all be enjoyed in a lovely courtyard at the back. ££

Demuths
2 North Parade Passage; tel: 01225 446059; www.demuths.co.uk; daily lunch and dinner.
A great restaurant, which happens to be vegetarian, serving light and fresh fare, such as shallot tatin with blue cheese mousse, and local organic food. Child friendly, relaxed atmosphere, good service. Winner of Bath Good Food Award for Best Vegetarian Restaurant 2012. ££–£££

Jamuna
9–10 High Street; tel: 01225 464631; www.jamuna-cuisine.com; daily lunch and dinner.
This family-run Indian restaurant offers good food with great views of the Abbey and Orange Grove. Traditional dishes include chicken or lamb tikka, tandoori fish and baltis. £–££

Roman Baths Kitchen
11–12 Abbey Churchyard; tel: 01225 477877; www.romanbathkitchen.co.uk; restaurant daily 8.30am–9/10pm, deli until 6pm.
Opened 2012 in a prime spot opposite the Roman Baths showcasing West Country produce. Eat in the simple bistro upstairs or grab a bite from the deli below. £–££

Salathai
14–15 Pierrepont Place; tel: 01225 484663; www.salathai-bath.co.uk; daily lunch and dinner.
Just a few minutes from the Abbey, this is a family-run restaurant offering stir-fries, curries and other delicious Thai specialities. ££

Sally Lunn's
4 North Parade Passage; tel: 01225 461634; www.sallylunns.co.uk; Mon–Sat 10am–9.30/10pm, Sun 11am–9pm.
This cosy restaurant serves traditional English food such as gammon hock served with a slice of Sally Lunn bun. Book in advance in the evening. £–££

Yak Yeti Yak
12 Pierrepont Street; tel: 01225 442299; www.yakyetiyak.co.uk; daily lunch and dinner.
Popular basement restaurant featuring authentic Nepalese cooking. Dishes include pork sag aloo and various dhals with a good range for vegetarians. Children welcome. ££

Tour 2

Georgian Grandeur
(The Upper Town)

See the best of Bath's Georgian architecture, including the
unforgettable Royal Crescent and Circus, on a 2-mile (3.2km)
walk that can fill a whole day if you take in all the sights

Bath is renowned for its Georgian
architecture and this route highlights the gems of the Upper Town, an
area that became increasingly fashionable as the 18th century went on. The
ideal place to start is Queen Square, a
short walk northwest of the Roman
Baths, because this was where John
Wood the elder, Bath's most influen-
tial architect, made his mark.

Highlights

- Queen Square
- The Circus
- Royal Crescent
- Royal Victoria Park
- Georgian Garden
- The Assembly Rooms
- The Fashion Museum

QUEEN SQUARE

Built between 1729 and 1739, **Queen
Square ❶** was Wood's first major
undertaking and was seminal to the
development in Bath of the Palladian
style, with its emphasis on propor-
tion, graceful lines and symmetry.

Built on the slopes north of the old
city, it was designed to look like a noble courtyard. Wood described it as
'soaring above the other buildings with
a sprightliness, which gives it the elegance and grandeur of the body of a

work by taking a home in the centre of the north range for himself.

The obelisk in the centre of the square is dedicated to Frederick Prince of Wales. It was erected by Beau Nash, in acknowledgement of a gold enamelled snuffbox which the 'King of Bath' had received from the Prince. The green space at the heart of the square, despite now being surrounded by traffic, is a popular outdoor spot for office workers and tourists to enjoy an alfresco lunch. It is also the site for an annual charity boules competition held each summer with 64 teams taking part.

The south side of the square, now home to the Francis Hotel, was damaged in the Baedeker bombing raids of 1942 (see box, p.33). Like many of the buildings that fell victim to the Luftwaffe in Bath, it was restored to its original design.

Just north of the square, at 40 Gay Street, is the **Jane Austen Centre** (tel: 01225 443000; www.jane austen.co.uk; daily Apr–Oct 9.45am– 5.30pm, until 7pm Thur–Sat July–Aug, Nov–Mar Sun–Fri 11am–4.30pm, Sat 9.45am–5.30pm; charge) which offers an introduction to Austen's association

Left: the magnificent Circus, the centrepiece of Georgian Bath. **Above**: the popular Jane Austen Centre.

stately palace'. The square's north side is especially striking, the Roman Portico uniting the terrace to palatial effect. Of all the terraces Wood designed, the north side of Queen Square is the finest. The rest of the buildings around the square were designed to be foils to the exquisite north side. The architect showed his pride in the

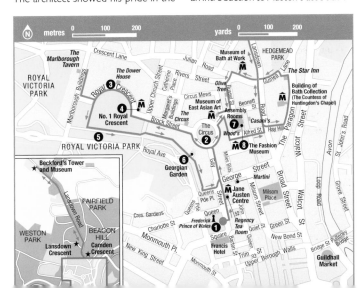

with Bath. In this Georgian town house, you can find out more about Bath in Austen's time and the importance of the city in her life and work. The exhibition has been created with the guidance of local members of the Jane Austen Society and authorities on the writer. The centre has knowledgeable staff, a period atmosphere, maps, books and exhibits on costumes and Austen film adaptations. It identifies the various Bath houses in which the author lodged or lived, including No. 25 Gay Street just up the hill, where she stayed for a few months following her father's death. You don't have to visit the exhibition at the centre to enter the tearooms *(see p.39)*. You can also join costumed guides on a tour of Austen's Bath.

Continue north up Gay Street, named after the landowner and speculator Robert Gay with who Wood collaborated on several building projects in the area. This street was extended to link with the Circus. The three-storey properties, home these days to a mix of accountants, solicitors and new technology companies, are plain ex-

cept for the eye-catching corner building with its ornate bow, which was once occupied by Wood the younger.

THE CIRCUS

Whether inspired by the Colosseum in Rome, or the ancient site of Stonehenge, or both (a matter of conjecture), **The Circus** ❷ was Britain's first circular street. The name comes from the Latin 'circus', which means a ring, oval or circle. The foundation stone was laid in February 1754 but Wood died a few months later, and the project was completed by his son. The Circus is a remarkable achievement. The three separate segments, with 33 houses in all, are separated by streets. From whatever direction you approach the Circus, you are faced with an uninterrupted sweep of buildings, with no gap to break the continuity. Note the architectural details: the acorns on the pediment, believed to allude to King Bladud *(see p.59)*; the decorative frieze depicting all the arts and trades of the day; and the Roman influence in the three types of column on the facade – Doric for the bottom

Below: a window tax imposed from 1696 to 1851 prompted residents to block up excess windows, an early form of tax avoidance.

Above: motifs depicting the arts, sciences and occupations are visible above the Doric columns of the Circus.

storey, Ionic for the middle, and Corinthian for the top, following the classical rules of architecture outlined by Palladio. As the houses are arranged in a circle, there is no central feature to detract from a continuous architectural pattern. Originally the area in the middle of the Circus, now graced by plane trees, was simply a cobbled space with nothing to obstruct the view of the buildings. Many famous people have lived on the Circus, including the statesmen William Pitt the Elder (Nos 7 and 8), Clive of India (No. 14) and the portrait painter Thomas Gainsborough (No. 17). More recently, one of the houses was owned by Hollywood superstar Nic Cage, who celebrated his association with his adopted city by switching on the Christmas lights in 2009. During the Baedeker Blitz of 1942, a bomb fell into the Circus, demolishing several of the houses, which were rebuilt after the war.

THE ROYAL CRESCENT

Like his father before him, John Wood the Younger also designed an architectural first. The **Royal Crescent** ❸ (1767–74) is a short walk west of the Circus, along the rather modest Brock Street, which was designed by Wood to supply an interval of repose between the splendid creations at each end. In a city graced with impressive streets and buildings, the Crescent is Bath's *pièce de résistance*. Walter Ison, an authority on Georgian architecture, described it as 'the greatest single achievement in the whole field of our urban architecture'. It occupies a dramatic position above Royal Victoria Park, its private lawn separated from the park by a ha-ha, giving the appearance of a seamless stretch of grass.

The Crescent's design consists of a great curve of 30 houses, almost 50ft (15m) high and more than 500ft (150m) in length. The Crescent is plainer than the Circus, with the only real decoration being the giant order of Ionic columns, 114 in all, providing a splendid uniformity. As you approach from Brock Street, it is impossible not to be blown away on first seeing it. The Crescent idea was copied several times in Bath and was adopted in many other British towns and cities, but this is the original and the best.

❻ Life in Georgian Bath

Privileged members of Georgian society would rise early to attend the baths. From 8am, they would visit the Pump Room, to be seen and to meet friends, drinking several glasses of spring water. Ladies would then head to their lodgings while men would visit libraries to read journals and discuss the news. At midday, it was the custom to attend church, with lunch usually at 3pm. The evening entertainments included concerts, gambling, dancing or attending plays.

Above: the grounds in front of the Royal Crescent make the perfect spot for a summer's picnic.

It's worth wandering up the side of Margaret's Buildings, to the east of the Crescent, with its eclectic mix of shops and restaurants (see p.36), to see Bath's dirty secret. While the front of the Crescent is magnificent, the back of the buildings is a real mish-mash. The front is completely uniform and symmetrical, whereas the rear is a mixture of differing roof heights as the developers were left to their own devices. This approach was common-place in Bath at the time and is known as 'Queen Anne fronts and Mary-Anne backs' architecture. Walking along the Crescent, you will see several plaques recalling famous past residents including Isaac Pitman (No. 17), the inventor of shorthand, and Elizabeth Linley (No. 11). The latter was the beautiful daughter of Thomas Linley, director of music at the Assembly Rooms. A gifted soprano, she was the darling of Bath in the 1770s, and painted by Gainsborough and Reynolds. Her engagement at the behest of her father to a wealthy but ageing suitor inspired The Maid of Bath, a satire by Samuel Foote.

Eventually released from the unhappy betrothal, she went on to elope with the young and dashing playwright Richard Sheridan, who wrote The Rivals.

The street was originally called just the Crescent, and the adjective Royal was added at the end of the 18th

Below: the Botanical Gardens in Victoria Park are home to tree and plant species from all over the world.

has doubled the number of rooms open to the public and created an extended historic house museum. Each room has been furnished as it might have been in the 18th century, offering an exquisite example of Georgian interior design with authentic furniture, painting, carpets and textiles. You get a glimpse of a typical bustling kitchen of the period, giving you an insight into how the Georgians used to entertain.

ROYAL VICTORIA PARK

In front of the Royal Crescent, **Royal Victoria Park ❺** sweeps downhill. Completed in 1830 and paid for by public subscription, the park was intended to provide space and fresh air in an increasingly built-up city. However, instead of providing recreation for everybody, it soon became the preserve of the middle classes, with wardens given the task of removing anyone regarded as unclean or undesirable. Happily, the park today is a vital and inviting space for the whole city. The obelisk on the west side of Marlborough Buildings, which dissects the park, records important episodes in the reign of Queen

century after Prince Frederick, Duke of York and Albany, had lived at Nos 1 and 16. In the 1970s, one resident, Miss Wellesley-Colley, painted her front door at No. 22 yellow instead of the traditional white. The Bath and North East Somerset council issued a notice insisting it should be repainted. A court case ensued that resulted in the Secretary of State for the Environment having to step in to declare that the door could remain yellow, resulting in a rare defeat for Bath's conservative planners.

No. 1 Royal Crescent

If you want to get a glimpse of how the Georgians lived in these splendid houses, you can visit **No. 1 Royal Crescent ❹** (tel: 01225 428126; Tue–Sun 10am–5.30pm, Mon noon–5.30pm, closed Mon except for Bank Holidays; charge), the home of John Wood the Younger's father-in-law, Thomas Brock, which has been turned into a museum. No. 1 re-opened its doors again in June 2013 following a major project to reunite its original 18th-century servants' wing with the rest of the house. The refurbishment

Below: No. 1 Royal Crescent offers a fascinating glimpse into Georgian life.

Victoria, who attended the opening of the park named in her honour as an 11-year-old girl in 1830. During the park's opening ceremony, a gust of wind blew her skirt in the air. Someone joked that she had fat legs, much to the public's amusement. Victoria was so upset by this that she never returned to Bath in her long life. While the park's eastern end offers bowling, tennis, putting and adventure golf (great for kids), the dells, pool, walkways and shrubberies of the Botanical Gardens on the western side conceal many delights – lichen-covered statues, a copy of the Temple of Minerva, a sundial, a dovecote and more.

GEORGIAN GARDEN

At the other end of the scale from Royal Victoria Park is the **Georgian Garden** ❻ (daily 9am–7pm, Nov–Mar until 4pm; free), off the Gravel Walk below the east side of the Royal Crescent. Excavations in 1985 to restore this walled garden behind No. 4 the Circus to its 18th-century state revealed original paths and flowerbeds. Planted with species typical of the Georgian era, it is restful in its symmetry and privacy, as well as allowing a glimpse of the Circus from the back. It's worth stopping to pause here to enjoy the serenity of the gar-

Above: practising a few steps in the Assembly Rooms' ballroom.

den amid the bustling city. At the end of the Gravel Walk turn left and left again to return to The Circus.

THE ASSEMBLY ROOMS

Chief among the attractions of the Upper Town in Georgian times were the **Assembly Rooms** ❼ (tel: 01225 477173; daily when not in use for private functions, Nov–Feb 10.30am–4pm, Mar–Oct 10.30am–5pm, last exit one hour after these times; free), in Bennett Street, on the east side of

❶ Royal Victoria Park

Royal Victoria Park, below the Crescent, is the perfect place for the children to let off steam after a sight-seeing session. There are lots of activities to entertain the kids, including a wonderful play area in the southwest corner that appeals to children of all ages. There's also a fun adventure golf course, tennis courts, a lake and a small aviary. It's also a favourite spot for families to chill out and enjoy a picnic.

Above: a blossoming picnic spot in Royal Victoria Park.

the Circus. These rooms were one of three sets in the city, the others being in the Lower Town. As the century went on there was quite a bit of rivalry between the upper and lower assemblies, and from 1777 they each had their own master of ceremonies. These rooms, the only ones still standing, were designed by John Wood the Younger in 1769. The necessary £20,000 was raised by 'tontine' subscriptions, whereby the shares of any shareholder that died were split between remaining members. Running costs and profits were met by subscriptions: one guinea allowed up to three people to attend the season's balls, but it was necessary to take out additional subscriptions to attend concerts or to play cards.

The rooms comprise a ballroom, the largest 18th-century building in Bath at 106ft (32m) long, the Octagon, a Card Room and a Tea Room. The ballroom is magnificent, graced by five cut-glass chandeliers. The plain area below the Corinthian columns around the wall was taken up by tiers of seating, with the front row reserved

F Baedeker Raids

Bath had been regarded as a relative haven during World War II but the peace was shattered during a series of raids in 1942. Launched in retaliation for RAF attacks on historic German cities, the raids targeted cultural cities, selected from a Baedeker guidebook. More than 400 people were killed and many buildings were damaged or destroyed.

for the belles of the ball and the rear for the plain or the elderly.

A ball was held once a week, beginning at 6pm with the highest-ranking lady present being led on to the floor for a minuet, which went on until 8pm, when the more energetic country dances commenced. At 9pm tea was served, followed by more dancing until 11pm. During this time non-dancers could play cards in the Octagon or, after it was added to the complex in 1777, the Card Room. Gambling was one of the chief pleasures of the

Above: the shop at the Fashion Museum offers an excellent collection of art and fashion books, cards and souvenirs.

Above: exhibits at the Fashion Museum chart fashion through the ages, from Georgian times to the present day.

Georgians. Beau Nash made his living from it, and laws curtailing gambling in 1739 and 1745 contributed to his eventual decline.

As the century wore on, private parties were preferred over public balls. In the 19th century the Upper Rooms declined, though not without flashes of their former glory when Johann Strauss and Franz Liszt performed and Charles Dickens gave public readings. In 1920, the rooms were converted into a cinema, and though restored by the National Trust in 1931 they were badly bombed during the Baedeker raids of 1942. Since then they have been restored to their former glory and evoke the elegance of the Georgian age.

FASHION MUSEUM

Downstairs is the **Fashion Museum** ❽ (tel: 01225 477789; www.fashion museum.co.uk; same opening times as the Assembly Rooms; charge). Originally known as the Museum of Costume, the attraction has undergone a transformation over the past decade, emerging with a more modish name and a concerted effort to make the museum more accessible and relevant to modern visitors. Temporary exhibitions have included a show featuring outfits worn by the Motown girl group The Supremes in the 1960s and 1970s, opened by Mary Wilson, one of the band's singers. There have also been shows focusing on 1977, when punk and new wave styles entered the mainstream, a retrospective of 1970s fashion designer Bill Gibb, costumes from Jane Austen productions as worn by Kate Winslet, Hugh Grant, Emma Thompson and Colin Firth, and an examination of one of the best-loved garments in any woman's wardrobe – the floral frock. Every year since 1963, a new outfit has been chosen to represent the year in fashion and added to the permanent collection so you can recall the fashion disasters of your youth, from padded shoulders to loon pants, Armani to Versace. There are also chances for children and grown-ups to try on hats, wigs, coats and other clothes from Georgian times.

Other collections show how the fashions of the past five centuries have

Above: each year a Dress of the Year is selected for display.

reflected their times – such as how powdered wigs suddenly went out of fashion in the 1790s when a new tax on powder was introduced to raise money for the wars with France, or how sober muslins became fashionable daywear in the wake of the French Revolution when signs of wealth needed to be concealed. The museum covers fashion from the 16th century to the present day, with some fascinating insights into Georgian society.

Exiting from the Assembly Rooms, turn left and then left again into Alfred Street where, at No. 14, you can see a full complement of original Georgian ironwork framing the entrance. It includes the horn-shaped snuffers in which sedan chairmen could extinguish their rag torches before going inside, a boot scrape, and a winch for delivering heavy goods such as wines to the cellar. Though the ironwork is painted black, as it is all over Bath today, in the 18th century it might have been grey, green or even blue.

CRESCENTS AND TOWERS

At the end of Alfred Street, a 10- to 15-minute walk up Lansdown Road leads to two handsome crescents, first the incomplete Camden Crescent, designed by John Eveleigh in 1788, and Lansdown Crescent, designed by John Palmer in 1789. Further north on top of Lansdown Hill (catch bus No. 2 or No. 702 to Ensleigh and then walk a short distance north along Lansdown Road) is **Beckford's Tower and Museum** (tel: 01225 460705; www.beckfords tower.org.uk; Apr–Oct Sat, Sun and Bank Holiday Mon 10.30am–5pm, last admission 4.30pm, weekdays by arrangement; charge), which is well worth a visit if you are here on the weekend. Built in 1827 as a study-retreat for William Beckford, better

Ⓥ Bath Balloon Flights

One of the most awe-inspiring sights on a beautiful summer's day is a view of a fleet of hot-air balloons soaring over the city's skyline. The balloon flights (see p.114) are usually launched from Royal Victoria Park in the early morning or early evening. If you can't afford to pay for a flight yourself, you can still watch the balloons as they go up and even lend a hand in getting them airborne.

Above: enjoy a bird's-eye view of the city from a hot-air balloon.

(S) Margaret's Buildings

The 'top of Bath' (Upper Town) is filled with hidden retail gems surrounded by beautiful Georgian architecture; places like Margaret's Buildings, a charming pedestrianised lane tucked away between the Royal Crescent and The Circus. This hidden gem offers a unique mix of irresistible boutiques, fine and contemporary art galleries, and antique and vintage clothing shops for you to explore. Lovers of antiquarian books should head for Bath Old Books at the very end.

known, perhaps, for Fonthill Abbey, his Gothic fantasy in Wiltshire, the tower offers views as far as the Forest of Dean, the Bristol Channel and Salisbury Plain from its gilded belvedere. Beckford, who inherited the estate at Fonthill plus £2 million in cash at the tender age of nine, was a flamboyant eccentric. He moved to Bath when the remodelling of Fonthill depleted his fortune and forced him to sell. The tower, which has been restored by the Bath Preservation Trust and taken on by the Landmark

Trust, formed the climax of a series of pleasure gardens that extended from his house in Lansdown Crescent. Beckford's tomb can be seen in the spooky cemetery adjoining the 120ft (37m) neoclassical tower, with its 156 steps. A footpath links the cemetery to the Blathwayt Arms pub in Lansdown, near the racecourse.

For those who want to get a sense of how Beckford lived, you can rent out the ground floor with access to the tower from the Landmark Trust and enjoy what Beckford called the 'finest prospect in Europe'.

GOTHIC CHAPEL

Back in the Upper Town, turn down Hay Hill from the end of Alfred Street to reach the Paragon. It was at No. 1 the Paragon that Jane Austen stayed on her first visit to Bath in 1797. The buildings flanking the near side of the road are known as the Vineyards, on account of the vines that flourished here until the land was developed in the 1760s.

A left turn here leads to the **Countess of Huntingdon's Chapel**. Selina Countess of Huntingdon (1707–91) was an aristocratic Methodist, who sold her jewels to raise money for the

Below: perched high above the city on Lansdown Hill, Beckford's Tower offers a spectacular panoramic view.

Above: the Paragon was designed by Thomas Warr Attwood, who sadly died in a building accident before the terrace was completed.

cause. This was the fourth chapel she built. John Wesley preached here on a number of occasions, 'attacking the devil in his own headquarters', as he saw it, and drew surprisingly large audiences. The presence of the Countess in Bath placed Beau Nash in a social quandary. Though he disliked the Methodists, and had several run-ins with them, his natural snobbery inclined him to kowtow to the Countess.

The **Building of Bath Collection** (see p.41) (tel: 01225 333895; http://buildingofbathcollection.org. uk; Tue–Fri 2–5pm, Sat–Sun 10.30am– 5pm, closed Dec–Jan; charge) housed within offers an illuminating account and gives a unique insight into the talents and techniques that created the lovely, seamless facades of Bath. Every aspect of building is covered, from the speculative deals that drove the building boom to the evolution of modern paints and wallpapers. For children, there's a dressing-up box and a Georgian wendy house.

Ⓕ Smelly Georgian Streets

At the back of the Circus, the night soilman used to collect waste from the privies before 5am, so the smell would be gone when the gentry awoke. The waste was dumped to the west of the Royal Crescent but the winds sometimes carried the smell to the posh homes. Supposedly, the houses on Marlborough Buildings were put up to block the smell. The land where the waste was deposited is now home to the city's most fertile allotments.

Above: the Circus attracted some unpleasant odours in Georgian times.

Above: the Museum of Bath at Work houses paraphernalia from the engineering workshops of local businessman J.B. Bowler.

MUSEUM OF BATH AT WORK

One of the city's more unusual museums is the Museum of Bath at Work (www.bath-at-work.org.uk; Apr–Oct daily 10.30am–5pm, Nov and Jan–Mar Sat–Sun 10.30am–5pm; charge); to get there return to Lansdown Road by cutting left past The Star Inn, then take Julian Road to Christ Church. Based upon the 'Bowler Collection', the eclectic contents of a 19th-century brass foundry and soda water factory, the museum recalls a largely forgotten industrial side to Bath. Jonathan Burdett Bowler was the archetypal small businessman,

who built up his engineering business through hard work and careful management. He adhered to two simple maxims: 'never throw anything away that might come in handy', and 'no job too large or small'. In 1877 he diversified into the manufacture and distribution of soda water using Bath's famous springs. The 19th-century store, engine room, workshops, office and factory have been reassembled here, uprooted from their original site in Corn Street in the Lower Town.

MUSEUM OF EAST ASIAN ART

From the museum, Russel Street leads back to Bennett Street and the Assembly Rooms. As you pass Circus Place, note the **Museum of East Asian Art** (tel: 01225 464640; www.meaa.org.uk; Tue–Sat 10am–5pm, Sun noon–5pm, last admission 4.30pm; charge), containing an exquisite collection of eastern antiquities and art treasures acquired by lawyer Brian S. McElney during his working life in Hong Kong. The museum offers lots of child-friendly activities such as mask-making and calligraphy.

From here, Gay Street will deliver you back to where this tour began.

Below: exquisite ceramics in the Museum of East Asian Art.

ⓔ Eating Out

Casani's
4 Saville Row; tel: 01225 780055;
www.casanis.co.uk; Tue–Sat lunch
and dinner.
This little corner of France in the
heart of Bath produces authentic
French cuisine with true Gallic flair.
It's on the small side so book if you
fancy classic French dishes perfectly
executed by renowned chef/patron
Laurent Couveur. £££

The Circus
34 Brock St; tel: 01225 466020; www.
thecircuscafeandrestaurant.co.uk;
Mon–Sat 10am–midnight (last orders
10.30pm).
Perfectly located between the
Circus and the Royal Crescent, this
family-run café and restaurant serving
'refined rustic British food' is popular
with both tourists and locals. ££

The Dower House
16 Royal Crescent; tel: 01225
823333; www.royalcrescent.co.uk;
daily lunch and dinner.
In the Royal Crescent Hotel, restaurants in Bath don't come any finer
than this. Accomplished chef David
Campbell works his magic in creating fab dishes and presentation is
key. Lavish surroundings do the food
justice. £££

The Marlborough Tavern
35 Marlborough Buildings; tel: 01225
423731; www.marlborough-tavern.
com; Mon–Sat lunch and dinner, Sun
lunch only.
The recipe for success here is simple:
great-tasting, home-cooked food
where the high-quality produce
speaks for itself, served in a welcoming pub atmosphere and backed
up with friendly, efficient service.
Outside they boast what is arguably
Bath's finest pub garden. ££

Martini
8–9 George Street; tel: 01225
460818; www.martinirestaurant.co.uk;
daily lunch and dinner.
Exuberant Italian restaurant run by
Italians. Deliciously sauced meat and

poultry, the freshest of fish, home-
made pastas, fabulous stone baked
pizzas and fine cheeses, all comple-
mented by ice creams as only the
Italians know how to make. ££

Olive Tree
4–7 Russel St; tel: 01225 447928;
www.olivetreebath.co.uk; Tue–Sun
lunch and dinner.
Consistently excellent modern British
cooking – pan-fried John Dory or
braised belly of pork – in an attractive
basement restaurant, part of the chic
Queensberry boutique hotel. Service
is usually sound. Good value at lunch
time. ££–£££

Regency Tea Room
40 Gay Street; tel: 01225 443000;
www.janeausten.co.uk/the-jane-austen-
centre/regencytearoom; daily Apr–Oct
9.45am–5.30pm, July–Aug Thur–Sat
until 7pm, Nov–Mar 11am–4.30pm.
Be refreshed with real leaf tea or
frothy coffee as well as a selection
of luscious cakes, served in a lovely
period atmosphere above the Jane
Austen Centre. £–££

The Star Inn
23 The Vineyards; tel: 01225 425072;
www.star-inn-bath.co.uk; Mon–Fri
noon–2.30pm and 5.30–11pm, Sat
noon–11pm; Sun noon–10.30pm.
OK, so there's no food worth speak-
ing of – unless you fancy a fresh roll
or a pickled egg – but this superb,
historic pub should not be missed.
Try the wonderful Bass ale served
from a jug or the local Bellringer bit-
ter, savour the atmosphere and the
unspoilt interior. £

Wood's
9–13 Alfred St; tel: 01225 314812;
www.woodsrestaurant.com; Mon–Sat
lunch and dinner.
This family-run place has been here
for more than 30 years. It offers good-
value (especially at lunch time) modern
British cooking – steamed mussels in
a white wine sauce or sea bream with
herb and caper beurre blanc – in a
lively, informal setting. ££–£££

Architectural Bath

Bath offers a unique architectural experience. Constructed on a grand scale, it has resulted in one of the most elegant cities in Europe and the finest Georgian city in Britain

BUILDING BOOM

The Bath we know and love today was largely the result of an unprecedented building boom that began in the early 18th century and lasted for almost 100 years. During that time, the city was graced with its glorious Georgian facades, producing breathtaking architecture such as the Royal Crescent, which has no equal in Britain. Few cities can match the harmony and scale of Bath's buildings, clad in the pale honey-coloured stone that seems

to glow in the sun. In spite of a series of bombing raids in World War II and some misguided post-war planning decisions, much of the Georgian city remains intact, providing an almost unprecedented living record of the Age of Elegance, with dazzling crescents, terraces and squares.

FAMILY BUSINESS

Much of the credit for the Bath we see today goes to the vision of the architect John Wood, who arrived in the city as it was taking off as a fashionable resort

The Building of Bath

For a deeper understanding of how Bath developed into such a unique city, head to the Building of Bath Collection. Housed in the Countess of Huntingdon's Chapel, ironically one of the few buildings in Bath done in the Gothic style rather than the predominant classical Palladian fashion, the museum offers an overview of the city's transformation from a provincial town into a world-renowned spa. The museum, owned and managed by the Bath Preservation Trust, houses a fully detailed architectural model of the historic city centre, giving an insight into the layout of Georgian Bath. Visitors can discover how the buildings were designed, built, decorated and lived in during the 18th century.

in the early 18th century. Wood came to Bath in 1725 with a grand scheme of how the city should be developed, based on the teachings and inspired by the great Italian architect, Andrea Palladio (1508–80). His interpretation of the classical Roman principles of architecture, known as the Palladian style, was adopted by travellers on the Grand Tour of Europe and became popular in Britain thanks to architects such as Inigo Jones, Lord Burlington, and John Wood himself.

Though Wood's grand vision of transforming Bath into the Rome of Britain was never fully realised, his genius can be seen in Queen Square *(see p.26)* and at Prior Park *(see p.64)*. Wood died in 1754 but his work was carried on by his son John Wood the Younger, who became every bit as impressive an architect as his father. He completed the work his father had begun on The Circus *(see p.28)*, which features 33 grand and elegantly proportioned houses in a circular arrangement, and then topped it with the Royal Crescent *(see p.29)*, a beautiful curving terrace. The crescent idea was copied several times in Bath and in other cities in Britain, but Wood's masterpiece remains the original and the best.

Other architectural gems include Pulteney Bridge and Great Pulteney Street *(see p.47)*, northwest of the Abbey; the Guildhall *(see p.42)*; the Assembly Rooms *(see p.32)*; and Lansdown and Camden crescents *(see p.35)* to the north.

Above: the Guildhall. **Top Right**: shops on Pulteney Bridge. **Bottom Right**: cast-iron lamp outside the Pump Room. **Left**: ornamental frieze supported by Doric columns in the Circus.

Tour 3

Across Pulteney Bridge

This tour (½ mile/1km) across the peerless Pulteney Bridge can take anything from an hour to all day, depending on how long you want to spend at each location

The tour begins at the Guildhall, a symbol of the growing power and wealth of the mercantile classes during the late 1700s, and ends at the delightful Sydney Gardens, home to one of Bath's great attractions, the Holburne Museum, a dizzying cornucopia of art and artefacts.

THE GUILDHALL

This **Guildhall** ❶ (Mon–Fri, 9am–5pm, free; some rooms may be closed due to private functions) was designed in the 1770s by architect Thomas Baldwin after much competition and council infighting to replace an earlier building of 1625 on a different site. The wings topped by decorative cupolas were added by John Brydon in 1891, more than a century later.

Highlights

• The Guildhall
• Victoria Art Gallery
• Parade Gardens
• Pulteney Bridge
• Great Pulteney Street
• Holburne Museum
• Sydney Gardens

The Banqueting Hall

Baldwin's great achievement in the Guildhall is the Banqueting Hall, one of the finest public rooms in Britain, which made the Guildhall a suitable place for balls and entertainment as well as being a seat of government. Forget about the uninspired interiors of most municipal buildings, this magnificent

the Assembly Rooms. The Banqueting Hall and anterooms, intended as 'assembly rooms' for the aldermen and their guests, rivalled the more exclusive Upper and Lower rooms in their magnificence. Portraits of famous Bath figures surround a large portrait of George III ('mad George') by the studio of Joshua Reynolds. Over one of the fireplaces is a portrait of Ralph Allen *(see p.8)*, by William Hoare. For details about these artworks and others in the Guildhall, pick up a leaflet or ask at reception. The Guildhall, as well as being home to council offices and the debating chamber, also hosts weddings and various events and festivals.

Left: view of the River Avon and Parade Gardens. **Above**: pointing the way to some of Bath's many sights.

Covered market

Next door to the Guildhall is the entrance to the covered market (Mon–Sat 8am–5.30pm). The site for the market is one of the longest-running shopping venues in Bath, serving the community for around 800 years and operating from its current venue in one form or another from at least the 16th century. As the **Guildhall Market** ❷, it came into existence in the 1770s and acquired its famous dome in 1863. More than half the market was lost in a redevelopment in the 1890s when the Guildhall was extended. Apart from the entrance doors on both sides, little

room belongs on a completely different level. Walter Ison, an expert on the architecture of Georgian Bath, described it as 'beyond any question the finest interior in Bath and a masterpiece of late 18th-century decoration'. The walls and ceilings in this beautifully proportioned room have a richness and variety not previously seen in the city and never since surpassed. The three great chandeliers are a match for, or arguably better than, those in

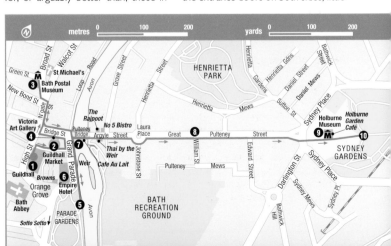

else remains of the 18th-century market except for the 'Nail', a stone pillar upon which market transactions used to take place.

The market is on the cheap and cheerful side but with several stalls, such as the hardware and electrical one, offering items that are difficult to find elsewhere in the city centre. You can also pick up reasonably priced jewellery, second-hand books, cheap greetings cards, and good-value fare from the deli stall. There's also a bakery, fruit and veg stall, café, fancy dress shop and a barber's.

BATH POSTAL MUSEUM

From the market entrance on High Street, head north to Northgate Street, where you will find the **Bath Postal Museum** ❸ (tel: 01225 460333; www.bathpostalmuseum.co.uk; Mon–Sat 11am–5pm, 4.30pm in winter; charge), in the same building as the city's central post office on the corner with Green Street. The museum's original home was on nearby Broad Street, where the world's first postage stamp, the Penny Black, was sent on 2 May 1840. Bath played a pivotal role in the development of the British postal system, thanks to the work of Ralph Allen who expanded established routes and stamped out corruption, and John Palmer, who improved efficiency with the introduction of mail coaches.

Exhibits track the development of the postal service and of the postbox, but also touch upon some delightful peripheral topics. You can explore the history of writing, listen to the experiences of postmen past and present and find out what life was like on board a Victorian mail coach or inside a re-created Victorian post office. There is a collection of early valentines and an 'address cabinet' of famous Bath residents, complete with portraits and biographical notes. It's fun for children, who can play the mail computer challenge and other interactive games, try on costumes, and perforate their own sheet of stamps. It also stocks items for the serious philatelist and would-be collectors.

VICTORIA ART GALLERY

Double back the way you came on High Street, turning left on to Bridge Street, towards Pulteney Bridge,

Below: an array of old postboxes at the Postal Museum.

ⓖ Bath in Bloom

As you admire the delightful floral displays in Parade Gardens, Royal Victoria Park, and the hanging boxes in Milsom Street and elsewhere in the city, you will have an understanding of the efforts needed to make Bath a perennial contender for the Britain in Bloom prize. It has scooped the regional prize numerous times since the competition was launched in 1964, also winning the national title as best small city more than a dozen times in that period.

Above: Bath is especially pretty during the Bath in Bloom competition.

where you will find the **Victoria Art Gallery** ❹ (tel: 01225 477233; www.victoriagal.org.uk; Tue–Fri and Sat 10am–5pm, Sun 1.30–5pm; free). Its permanent collection, spread over two rooms on the first floor, has paintings from the 15th century to the present day, featuring artists with links to Bath. It includes Turner's *West Front of Bath Abbey*, *Adoration of the Magi*, attributed to Hugo Van der Goes, portraits by Zoffany and Gainsborough, a Whistler and several works by Walter Sickert. Also of interest is the collection of coloured glass perfume bottles and drinking glasses. At the foot of the impressive staircase is a fun 19th-century toy, which you can set in motion with a piece of small change. The cost can add up if you have small children as they can't seem to get enough of it.

There are also temporary exhibitions on the ground floor, including an annual show by the Bath Society of Artists. For children, there are special activities with worksheets and art trolleys stocked with a range of materials, while you can relax with a cup of tea or visit the small shop.

The gallery was named to mark Queen Victoria's 60 years on the throne and features a sculpture of the monarch outside and a frieze of classical figures.

PARADE GARDENS

From the Victoria Art Gallery, before heading on to Pulteney Bridge, take a detour on the right to Grand Parade, which offers picture-postcard views of the bridge and the weir *(see p.60)*

Below: the permanent collection at the Victoria Art Gallery.

Above: the graceful Italianate architecture of Pulteney Bridge is lit up at night.

and, further down, **Parade Gardens** ❺ (Apr–Sept; charge; free to Bath residents). The gardens, with their beautiful and elaborate floral displays, deckchairs, and brass band performances on summer Sundays, are a very popular place to unwind when the weather's fine. In the gardens, you will also find statues of Mozart and of Prince Bladud, legendary founder of Bath. Nearby are North and South parades (both designed by John Wood the Elder).

> ### Ⓕ Film Location
>
> A taste of Hollywood came to Bath in October 2012 when filming for the movie version of the West End musical *Les Miserables* took place at Pulteney Weir. Crews captured shots that included a stunt man jumping into the River Avon from Grand Parade, which is believed to be from a spectacular scene at the end of the film where actor Russell Crowe's character, Inspector Javert, commits suicide by jumping into the River Seine.

EMPIRE HOTEL

Looming over Parade Gardens is the **Empire Hotel** ❻, one of the most controversial buildings in Bath. The Empire was built in 1901 by city architect Major Charles Edward Davis, the man who uncovered the Great Bath. The architecture of the roof is supposed to reflect the three classes of people, with a castle keep on one corner for the upper class, a Dutch gable-style house for the middle classes and a country cottage for the lower classes. Richard Morriss, in his book *The Buildings of Bath*, calls it a monstrosity: 'stylistically bizarre and far too big for its prominent position between the abbey and the river'. Nonetheless, the Empire still holds a place in the heart of some Bathonians. The hotel was taken over during World War II by the Admiralty, despite Bath's lack of proximity to the sea, and went on to house Ministry of Defence offices long after the war. In the 1990s, the building was transformed into exclusive apartments for over-55s. If you walk down the east side of the hotel, you can see the back of the Guildhall. Take a close look at the middle window, which is artificial

and designed to maintain the building's symmetry, masking a chimney shaft running up the middle of the Guildhall.

PULTENEY BRIDGE

Inspired by the Ponte Vecchio in Florence and the Rialto in Venice, **Pulteney Bridge** ❼ was commissioned by William Johnstone Pulteney and designed by Robert Adam between 1770 and 1774. It cost a then astonishing £11,000 to build, not least on account of the tiny shops lining both sides. The bridge is both lovely and unique, retaining its grace and charm in spite of later alterations and the clutter of modern shop fronts. The tall Venetian windows, the dominant central feature, are balanced by domed pavilions at each end. It remains one of only four bridges in the world with shops on both sides. The bridge, brilliantly inventive and elegant, paved the way for the development of Bathwick (an estate owned by Pulteney), under the direction of the young Thomas Baldwin, the architect of the Guildhall (see p.42). The south side of the bridge was restored to its original glory in 1975, when outbuildings defacing its flat front were demolished. Less

elegant, however, is the back. Views from the Podium shopping centre or from the river show it is still overhung with back kitchens and store rooms.

GREAT PULTENEY STREET

Carry on over the bridge to Laura Place with its enticing fountain. From there, **Great Pulteney Street** ❽ sweeps down to Sydney Gardens and the Holburne Museum, providing a magnificent vista. This imposing street was designed by Thomas Baldwin in the late 1780s, incorporating elements of a previous design by Robert Adam, Pulteney's original choice of architect. The Bathwick project was interrupted by the economic slump of the 1790s and the huge array of crescents and terraces that Baldwin envisaged fanning out from Great Pulteney Street was never fully realised. The French Revolution caused shockwaves in the financial markets, banks collapsed and

---

Ⓢ EP Mallory & Son

Behind the elegant facade on the corner of Bridge Street is a family business with roots that go back over four generations, having been established in 1898. Fine jewellery has always been at the heart of this business, having its own workshops to produce bespoke items.

Above: diamond-encrusted ring for sale.

Above: Sydney Gardens backs onto the Kennet and Avon Canal towpath which can be joined at several points between Widcombe and Bathampton.

Bath's speculative developments came to a sudden halt, leading to many bankruptcies. Nonetheless, the street was a fashionable address in the late 18th and early 19th centuries, as the many plaques testify. William Wilberforce (1759–1833) stayed at No. 36; Emma Hamilton at No. 72; and Thomas Baldwin himself lived at No. 6. It was also a fitting home for the exiled French monarchy in the wake of the revolution. Also here and in Laura Place are examples of the six-sided letter boxes known as Penfold boxes, after their designer J.W. Penfold, which were used for a short while in the mid-19th century until their hexagonal design was found to trap letters – a reminder that style over content is not just a modern trend.

THE HOLBURNE MUSEUM

Based upon the collection of Sir Thomas Holburne (1793–1874), the **Holburne Museum** ❾ (tel: 01225 388569; www.holburne.org; daily 10am–5pm, Sun from 11am; free) is devoted to decorative and fine art of the 17th and 18th centuries, including paintings, silver, porcelain, miniatures, glass and furniture. Among the paintings are works by Turner, Stubbs, Gainsborough and Brueghel. Gainsborough made his name in Bath, painting the portraits of the famous. His rapid success can be gauged by his escalating fees, beginning at a modest 5 guineas in 1760 and rising to 100 guineas in around 1774. The museum reopened in 2011 following the completion of a bold glass extension to the rear that has doubled the gallery space and houses a garden café.

Ⓖ Railway Path

A 13-mile (22km) off-road route from Pulteney Bridge to St Philips Road in Bristol, the Bristol to Bath Railway Path was the first major project undertaken by cycling charity Sustrans. The path is open to walkers and cyclists, with access for disabled users. It's a lovely, flat ride through beautiful countryside and passes Bitton Station, where steam trains run on summer weekends. There's a sculpture park and other artworks on the route.

SYDNEY GARDENS

Sydney Gardens ❿ attracted 4,000 visitors a day during its glory years in Jane Austen's time. Later, in the 19th century, they were used for balloon ascents. Dissecting the gardens are Brunel's Great Western Railway (1840–41) and the Kennet and Avon Canal (opened 1810), industrial additions that were elegantly incorporated by means of landscaped cuttings and pretty stone and cast-iron bridges. Other attractions include a mock temple, based on the one that existed as part of the Roman Baths complex. Along with a chance to watch the trains as they whiz through, there are also tennis courts, a bowling green and a kiosk selling drinks and ice creams. From here, you can retrace your steps back to the centre of Bath.

Ⓔ Eating Out

Browns
Orange Grove; tel: 01225 461199; www.browns-restaurants.co.uk; daily lunch and dinner.
Quality, classic food served in elegant Georgian surroundings with a genteel yet cosmopolitan feel. The restaurant is spread over two floors with superb views out of the large windows from the graceful mezzanine. ££

Cafe au Lait
7 Pulteney Bridge; tel: 01225 338007; daily 8.30am–6pm.
It's worth making the effort to walk down to Pulteney Bridge for what, many claim, is the best cup of coffee in Bath. They also have lots of lovely cakes to choose from plus a good range of food. Nice relaxed environment with polite staff. £

Holburne Garden Café
Great Pulteney Street; tel: 01225 388569; www.holburne.org/garden-cafe; Mon–Sat 10am–5pm, Sun from 11am.
Housed in a huge glass extension to the Holburne Museum, natural materials – from wooden panelling to slate flooring and green tinted ceiling tiles – create the impression that you're eating outside amongst Sydney Gardens. A changing menu features interesting light lunches, sandwiches and cakes. £

No 5 Bistro
5 Argyle Street; tel: 01225 444499; http://no5bistro.co.uk; daily lunch and dinner.
Traditional French cuisine from a very talented chef. Simple but well-executed dishes include oven-baked snails and wild mushroom risotto. Live jazz Tue and Thur. ££–£££

The Rajpoot
4 Argyle Street; tel: 01225 466833; www.rajpoot.com; daily lunch and dinner.
Popular Indian that has won a host of British Curry awards. It offers Tandoori, Mughal and Bengali dishes, such as marinated rainbow trout and tandoori chicken, in a traditional setting. ££

Sotto Sotto
10 North Parade; tel: 01225 330236; http://sottosotto.co.uk; daily lunch and dinner.
Descend the stairs to this beautiful cellar restaurant, softly lit to accentuate the arches and bare stone walls. Simple cooking relying on quality ingredients is the key to the traditional Italian food with a contemporary twist. ££

Thai by the Weir
16 Argyle Street; tel: 01225 444834; www.thaibytheweir.co.uk; daily lunch and dinner.
The menu is packed with Thai delights, including tempura, tom yam soup and wok-fried noodles. Tables at the rear of this bustling restaurant have great views of the weir. £–££

Tour 4

The Spine of the City

This 1½-mile (2.5km) tour highlights the city's medical, scientific and theatrical links. There are plenty of shops en route so it could take anything from an hour to a full day

Compact, diverse and with a number of luxury shops not normally found outside London, Bath has the best shopping centre in southwest England and has done for centuries, with several of Jane Austen's characters depicted shopping in its lanes.

SOUTHGATE CENTRE

This walk starts in the south of the city near its railway station, at the recently completed **SouthGate Centre ❶**. Like any modern development in Bath, it has been dogged with controversy. For decades, the south end of Bath had been blighted by an unimpressive 1960s-built development that, while clad in the familiar Bath stone, was completely devoid of charm. In 2006, work began on de-

molishing the original shopping centre and replacing it with a more aesthetically pleasing, albeit predictably conservative, faux Georgian development. Despite concern over the site's lack of originality and anger over the demolition of the well-loved Churchill House to make way for a modern bus station with its bizarre-looking

Left: Milsom Street.

tower at one end, the new centre has been generally well received as an improvement on its largely unlamented predecessor.

STALL STREET

As you head north through the new centre, with its Debenhams department store, cafés, trendy clothing retailers and hip Apple store, you reach Stall Street, anchored by Marks & Spencer at the bottom. Stall Street was built by the architect John Palmer between the 1790s and 1800s. The structures have listed building status and are now occupied by shops and offices, and the location is a popular spot for buskers.

Head west on Westgate Street, home to Komedia, a comedy club and live entertainment venue *(see p.122)*, and cross over to Kingsmead

Square. On the square is Rosewell House, built in 1735 by John Strahan of Bristol for Thomas Rosewell and identified by the ornate, decorative carvings festooning the central window. Though Baroque architecture dominated continental cities in the 17th and early 18th centuries, this is the only Baroque building in Bath.

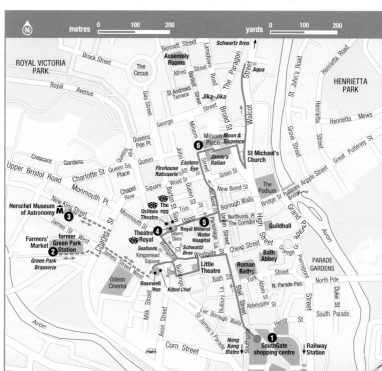

Above: the Theatre Royal opened in 1805 with a production of *Richard III*.

FARMERS' MARKET

If you want, you can take a short detour here to explore the Green Park development and the Herschel Museum. Exit the square in the southwest corner, go west on James Street West, past the Odeon multi-screen cinema, to explore the former Green Park railway station. The facade hides a fine iron train shed with a main roof span of 66ft (20m). Train services stopped in 1966 and the station became a car park. In a good example of a redundant building being adapted for a new purpose, it has been redeveloped to house a Sainsbury's supermarket, the largest in the city centre, and an excellent **Farmers' Market ❷** on Saturdays (9am–1.30pm). Such markets are now fairly commonplace, but, when launched in 1997, this one was the first in the country, heralding the revival of interest in locally grown, locally sourced and organic foods. Still thriving today, it features quality, fresh, seasonal produce at a fair price. The goods are sold directly by the people who produce them and everything comes from within a 40-mile (64km) radius of Bath. There is a range of stalls selling seasonal organic and non-organic fruit and vegetables, meat, fish, bread, cheese, savoury pies, cakes and soups.

HERSCHEL MUSEUM OF ASTRONOMY

As you leave the front of Green Park, home to the Green Park Brasserie, head east, crossing James Street West into Charles Street, and turning left into New King Street for the **Herschel Museum of Astronomy ❸** (tel: 01225 446865; www.herschel museum.org.uk; Mon–Fri 1–5pm, Sat–Sun 11am–5pm; charge), the house and observatory of William Herschel, an amateur astronomer who discovered Uranus in 1781. Herschel came to Bath from Hanover in 1761 and became musical director of the Assembly Rooms. But his abiding love was stargazing and he would hurry home from concerts to study the skies with the help of home-made telescopes. It was from the garden of this house that he discovered Uranus, adding to the number of known planets for the first time since antiquity. After his find, Herschel was made director of the Royal Astronomical Observatory. The museum features a short award-winning film narrated by the late Sir Patrick Moore, amateur astronomer and TV presenter, and you can see the workshop where Herschel built his telescopes and a replica of the one with which he discovered Uranus.

LITTLE THEATRE

From the museum, retrace your steps to Kingsmead Square, and take a short detour to the **Little Theatre** in St Michael's Place, the city's main venue for arthouse films. The cinema, which has been part of the Bath scene for more than 70 years, was the UK's oldest surviving independent cinema until 2012 when it was sold to the Cineworld group. Haile Selassie, the exiled emperor of Ethiopia, used to visit the cinema in the late 1930s to watch newsreels of the invasion of his country by Italian forces. The cinema was featured in animated form in the 2009 film *Fantastic Mr Fox* after its director Wes Anderson spotted the building during a trip to the city and decided it had the perfect look for his film.

Below: catching up on the local news.

THEATRE ROYAL

Head north up the alley beside the Grapes pub, which takes you on to Westgate Street. Go left and follow the curve of the road to the **Theatre Royal** ❹ in Saw Close, one of the oldest and most beautiful theatres in Britain. It has been the hub of Bath's thriving theatre scene from 1805, when the hitherto renowned Orchard Street Theatre moved here. Alongside the weekly touring productions that make up the majority of the Theatre Royal's programme, the venue is host to several festivals each year, including the Bath Shakespeare Unplugged, the Family Theatre Festival and a regular summer season by acclaimed director Peter Hall. Many plays start their run

Ⓢ Cheese Shops

Bath is blessed with two great cheese shops. The Fine Cheese Company at 29–31 Walcot Street has the edge with an outstanding selection of cheeses, plus delicious breads, olives, salami and other treats, as well as a good café. Staff are enthusiastic and well informed. It's a small shop, though, and can be busy. Paxton & Whitfield on John Street is also impressive, with an excellent range of cheeses.

Above: a fine selection of cheeses at Paxton & Whitfield.

Above: the Min is now a specialist hospital for rheumatic diseases.

at the Theatre Royal before their official opening in London, and Al Pacino, Charlton Heston, Vanessa Redgrave and Sir Ian McKellen are among the stars to have performed there. Even if you're not overly interested in seeing a production, it's worth taking a tour for a glimpse backstage behind the scenes and for a chance to view the interior. The auditorium has tiers of ornate plasterwork, with sumptuous red and gilt decoration, a majestic trompe l'œil ceiling and glittering chandelier. The theatre itself is said to be haunted by the Grey Lady, who was an actress centuries ago. She has been seen watching productions in the popularly named Grey Lady Box and supposedly leaves the distinctive scent of jasmine.

THE EGG

In 1997 a studio theatre was built at the rear of the building on Monmouth Street, called the **Ustinov Studio**, named after actor Peter Ustinov. It is the venue for an eclectic range of drama, dance and classical music.

In 2005 another new theatre was opened behind the Theatre Royal, the egg, which is a children's theatre, providing professional productions for children and their families, alongside workshops and youth theatre productions (see box, opposite).

In Seven Dials, a small square close to the theatre, the handprints of British actors and actresses, including John Gielgud, Joan Collins and Derek Jacobi, are cast in bronze around a fountain.

Next to the theatre is the house

Ⓢ Independent Bookshops

Book-lovers are spoilt for choice. The large Waterstone's on Milsom Street does a good job but has stiff competition from two outstanding independents. Mr B's Emporium of Reading Delights at 14/15 John Street, with its keen and committed staff, has been voted Britain's Independent Bookshop of the Year, while Toppings on the Paragon also has friendly and informed staff. It's worth signing up for one of Mr B's book spas, where you'll discover great reads you never knew existed.

(now the Strada restaurant) in which master of ceremonies Beau Nash died in 1761, tended by his mistress Juliana Popjoy. He lived here, next door to the home he occupied during the height of his success, for the last 16 years of his life, surviving on a pension of just £10 a month. One of the 'windows' above the restaurant is a trompe l'œil.

THE MIN

From here, Barton Street leads up to Queen Square, the start of Tour 2 (see p.26–39), but instead turn right along Upper Borough Walls to reach **The Royal Mineral Water Hospital ❺**. Known locally as the Min, this was a philanthropic venture built on the site of a theatre by John Wood the Elder between 1738 and 1742, under the collective auspices of Dr William Oliver of Bath Oliver biscuit fame, Ralph Allen, who provided the stone, and Beau Nash, who raised funds for the project. Ongoing expenses were met by fines levied on illegal gambling and by collections at church services. The extension to the hospital has a statue of the Good Samaritan in the pediment to reflect their philanthropic largesse, while the original building has a royal coat of arms.

The hospital used to cater for impoverished patients whose diseases were amenable to treatment by the Bath waters. Patients came from all over the country and had to pay a £3 deposit, either to fund their return trip home or to cover the cost of their funeral. The Royal National Hospital for Rheumatic Diseases, as it is now known, no longer offers mineral water therapy and is now a specialist hospital with an international reputation for its research and rehabilitation work. Though still a working hospital, you can ask at the main reception desk on the ground floor (small groups only) if it is possible to view parts of a Roman mosaic

Ⓚ The egg

The egg is the Theatre Royal's award-winning theatre dedicated to children and their families and was specifically designed with youngsters in mind. The café (with plenty of pushchair space) has a playhouse and lots of space for kids to run around, and the theatre hosts workshops and performances for babies and younger children year-round.

floor that were uncovered during work on the hospital. Opposite the hospital, below part of the remaining city wall, is a plaque marking the location of a cemetery where those who died in the hospital were buried.

MILSOM STREET

South of the Min is Union Street with its range of popular stores, but more interesting is the maze of smaller shops found in the alleys off the main drag, such as Northumberland Place, home to Bath's smallest pub, the Coeur du Lion, and the Corridor, a covered shopping arcade that opened in 1825. In 1974, the Corridor was renovated after suffering extensive damage from an Irish Republican Army bomb.

Heading north from the Min, Old Bond Street leads up to **Milsom Street ❻**, Bath's most famous shop-

Below: a memorial to the self-proclaimed 'King of Bath'.

IN THIS HOUSE RESIDED THE CELEBRATED *BEAU* NASH AND HERE HE DIED FEBY 1761

Bath Aqua Glass

Bath Aqua Glass takes its name from the city's latin title (Aquae Sulis). The distinctive blue colour is made by adding copper oxide to molten glass to give the aquamarine hue reminiscent of Bath's spa waters. At the shop in Walcot Street you can see glassware being made entirely by hand using traditional techniques. Have a go yourself and create your own bauble to keep (www.bathaquaglass.com; demonstrations Mon–Fri 11.15am and 2.15pm, Sat 2.15pm only).

ping street, laid out in the 1760s. The buildings were originally grand town houses with mansard roofs and Corinthian columns. As Milsom Street was situated between the old city and the new Upper Town, it quickly emerged as the most fashionable of shopping streets, a reputation that it still maintains today. Among the chic shops is the Octagon Chapel, which was designed in 1767 as a proprietary (subscription) chapel with fireplaces, carpets and 'every accommodation of ease and refinement'. The dominant shop on the street is the department store Jollys, part of the House of Fraser Group, which has been a Bath fixture since 1831.

Just off Milsom Street is a development called Milsom Place, an area comprised of stylish shops, with an emphasis on fashionable clothes and jewellery, and places to eat, such as Jamie Oliver's Italian restaurant. As you pass through Milsom Place with its boutiques offering designer clothes and other stylish goodies, you emerge on to Broad Street. Head south until you see St Michael's Church. Opposite is the former Podium shopping centre, where the ground floor is now fully occupied by a Waitrose supermarket and upstairs is the city's main library and a café.

WALCOT STREET

Keeping the Podium on your right, head north up **Walcot Street**. With its eclectic and quirky mix of independent shops, this contrasts with the rather slick and trendy Milsom Place. Walcot Street has long been home to Bath's artisans and specialist shops. Among the stores worth checking out are the British Hatter at No. 9, wholefood shop Harvest (37), Scandinavian furniture store Shannon (68) and Bath Aqua Glass (105), a glassblowing workshop and store. At 109, in historic Walcot Yard, is the wonderful MASCo at Walcot, a great place to view and buy salvaged architectural artefacts for the home and garden. A salvage business has been running on the site in one form or another since 1977.

Retrace your steps along Walcot Street to return to the city centre.

Left: classical garden statue on sale at MASCo at Walcot.

ⓔ Eating Out

Aqua
88 Walcot Street; 01225 471371; www.aqua-restaurant.com; daily lunch and dinner.

A beautifully restored chapel creates a cool, chic ambience in which to dine on first-rate Italian food. The fixed-price menu represents excellent value. Service is impeccable without being intrusive. ££

Eastern Eye
8a Quiet Street; tel: 01225 422323; www.easterneye.com; daily lunch and dinner.

This family-run Indian has been a long-time favourite in Bath, scooping many awards since it opened in 1983 in a dazzling Georgian setting, under a triple-domed vaulted ceiling, just off Milsom Street. ££

Firehouse Rotisserie
2 John Street; tel: 01225 482070; www.firehouserotisserie.co.uk; daily lunch and dinner.

Voted by Channel 4 as one of the five best American restaurants in the UK. It offers California-style roasted meats, seafood and gourmet pizzas with an open kitchen as the focal point. Lively atmosphere. ££

Hong Kong Bistro
33 Southgate; tel: 01225 316088; daily lunch and dinner.

The decor is unexciting, but the food at this Chinese restaurant cum noodle bar is excellent value and always reliable. There's an exhaustive menu with lots of authentic Chinese classics. Speedy service. £–££

Jamie's Italian
10 Milsom Place; tel: 01225 432340; www.jamieoliver.com/italian/bath; daily lunch and dinner.

This part of the Jamie Oliver empire serves very good rustic Italian food that introduces a nice combination of flavours, at not unreasonable prices. It has a buzzy authentic Italian atmosphere with fresh bread, meats and vegetables hanging on view in the kitchen. ££–£££

Jika-Jika
4a Princes Buildings, George Street; tel: 01225 429903; www.jikajika.co.uk; daily 8–9am–5–6pm (Wed and Fri until 11pm).

Excellent coffee from trained baristas and lovely breakfasts at this coffee house and canteen. Offers light meals, salads, ciabattas and daily hot specials. Child-friendly. £–££

Kilted Chef
7a Kingsmead Square; tel: 01225 466688; www.kiltedchef.co.uk; Wed–Sun lunch and dinner.

Haggis does appear on the menu but images of bagpipers and tartan are soon banished as you descend the stone steps to the contemporary vaulted dining room. Only opened in 2012, the Scottish menu put together by an award-winning chef is already pulling in a crowd. ££–£££

Moon & Sixpence
27 Milsom Place; tel: 01225 320080; www.moonandsixpence.co.uk; daily lunch and dinner.

When Milsom Place was redeveloped, this Bath standby emerged transformed with a funky new interior but with its reputation for excellent food intact. It serves modern, and sometimes inventive, international cuisine. £££

Schwartz Bros
4 Sawclose, tel: 01225 461726, and 102 Walcot Street, tel: 01225 463613; daily noon–11.30pm, with exceptions. If burgers aren't normally your thing, consider making an exception for this place whose burgers put the big chains to shame. Veggie options. £

Seafoods
38 Kingsmead Square; tel: 01225 465190; www.seafoodsfishandchips.co.uk; Mon–Wed 11.30am–9pm, Thur–Sat 11.30am–10pm, Sun noon–7pm.

The last surviving honest-to-goodness chippie in the city centre. Get them to go or eat inside with a nice cup of tea or a glass of beer or wine. £

Bath as a Spa

From the huge complex of baths and temples established by the Romans to the new spa facilities built 2,000 years later, Bath's *raison d'être* has always been its natural spring waters

The Roman city of Aquae Sulis, named after the Celtic goddess of hot springs, was founded to take advantage of the healing power of the waters. More than a million litres of mineral rich water at a temperature of 46°C (115°F) rise from three springs – the King's Bath, the Hot Bath and the Cross Bath – in the heart of Bath every day.

After the Romans left Britain, the complex gradually fell into decline and the Great Bath was only uncovered again by chance in 1880. The Great

Bath now forms the heart of the popular Roman Baths Museum, which attracts more than a million visitors a year.

GEORGIAN SPLENDOUR

The city's reputation as a spa was also one of the reasons why Bath became the most fashionable destination in the country outside London. This was partly inspired by the patronage of Princess Anne, who later became Queen. From 1688, she made a number of visits to the city, taking the waters and giving

Legend of Prince Bladud

Bath's spring waters made their mark long before the Romans, according to myth. In about 800BC, Prince Bladud, son of the king of Britain, was exiled when he contracted leprosy and was forced to live in isolation as a swineherd. One day his pigs, which had also caught the disease, started to roll in muddy water and found their skin was cleansed and cured. Bladud, hoping the waters would have the same effect, followed their example. Revitalised, he returned to his father's court and went on to build baths near the springs, laying the foundations for a temple around which the city grew. The legend of Bladud, the father of King Lear, who was immortalised by Shakespeare, is commemorated with a statue at the King's Bath, dating from 1699. A more modern statue of Bladud was placed in Parade Gardens in 2009 as part of a charity public art event celebrating Bath and its origins.

MODERN COMFORTS

To enjoy the spa waters today, you have to travel about 200 metres in distance from the Roman Baths and 2,000 years in time. The Thermae Bath Spa facility finally opened in 2006 after many delays and cost over-runs, combining the restoration of historic buildings with a new state-of-the-art leisure complex. The building, in glass and Bath stone, was designed by architects Nicholas Grimshaw & Partners and is the only place in the UK where you can bathe in natural, hot spring water.

The spa, offering more than 50 treatments, is spread over three floors and the high point, both literally and figuratively, is the open-air roof-top pool. Submerged under the hot mineral water, you can gaze across the Bath skyline – a magical experience, especially after dark.

Bath her royal seal of approval. Wherever the court went, the crowds followed. Bath's population grew from just over 2,000 at the beginning of the 18th century to 28,000 by 1801. This rise in popularity was accompanied by an improvement in the amenities and an unprecedented building boom, which created for the dazzling city enjoyed by millions of tourists every year.

Above: the Gorgon's head crowned the temple built by the Romans in AD43. **Top Left**: old and new – the Cross Bath and the New Royal Bath. **Centre Left**: Sulis Minerva, the goddess of healing. **Left**: a summer's evening at the Great Bath.

Tour 5

From Pulteney Bridge
to Prior Park

This 2½-mile (4km) round trip from Pulteney Weir, taking
in the National Trust-owned grounds of Prior Park and
views of the city, river and canal, will take around half a day

This walking tour begins at Pulteney Bridge *(see p.47)*, highlight-
ing some of the attractions along the
river and the Kennet and Avon Canal,
before heading south through Widcombe and up the hill to Prior Park.

Highlights
- Pulteney Weir
- River Avon
- Kennet and Avon Canal
- Bath Abbey Cemetery
- Prior Park

PULTENEY WEIR

Take the steps down at the north end
of the bridge leading to the **River
Avon**, passing the tiny Riverside Café
(see p.67), with its views of the bridge
and **Pulteney Weir** ❶. There were
older versions of the weir but this one
was built in the early 1970s. Alongside
the less lovely sluice and radial gate,
it's part of the city's flood control
measures, but despite its prosaic role

it still remains a thing of beauty. The
V-shape allows more water in than
a traditional diagonal one. The weir
serves as a starting point for some of
the river cruises on the Avon.

RECREATION GROUND

Heading south on the riverside path,
there's a large beer garden, part of the

Left: Pulteney Weir and canoeists on the River Avon. **Above**: narrowboat on the Kennet and Avon Canal.

Boater pub, which gets very crowded on rugby match days. Continue to the **Recreation Ground ❷**, known by all as the Rec, which is presently home to the city's Premier League rugby club – one of the most successful in English rugby history – as well as being an open space used by the public. The ground, with its riverside setting and view of the Abbey, is widely regarded as the most picturesque in the country. Its future has been uncertain but plans are on-going to increase capacity, but this is subject to legal processes and may take some time to come to fruition. Bath is a city where the oval ball comes first, as you will discover if you try to seek out a pub showing football when a major rugby contest is underway. There's a footpath through the Rec, so, unless there's a game on, you can wander in and check out the pitch and the other green spaces, which are used as a venue for summer music concerts, county cricket, and the annual bonfire night fireworks display among other events.

❻ Multi-purpose Weir

Originally designed in the 1970s as an answer to Bath's long history of devastating floods, Pulteney Weir is now being proposed as a possible source of hydro-electric power. The River Regeneration Trust is considering using that source of energy to power the Bath Christmas lights.

Above: view of the weir.

VIEW OF PULTENEY BRIDGE

Returning to the path, you will see narrowboats moored along the river opposite the city's main leisure

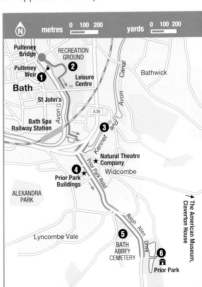

Above: narrowboats offer a leisurely way to enjoy the scenery around Bath.

centre *(see p.115)*. There is also an active zone for children, including a soft play area for toddlers. Walk up a set of stairs leading to the road bridge on Grand Parade if you want to look back at the picturesque view of Pulteney Bridge and the weir. The stairs, part of a former tollbooth, usually have the whiff of a public convenience about them. Otherwise, stay on the path by the river, passing the cricket ground on the left and St John's Catholic Church on the opposite bank. You may see someone with a telescope or binoculars trying to get a glimpse of the peregrine falcons that nest in the church steeple. Cross over the road at Spring Gardens, keeping the river on your right, passing under one of the railway bridges designed by the great

engineer Isambard Kingdom Brunel, when he brought the railways to Bath in 1840. As you walk on you will see where the canal joins the river. Glance over to your right at Halfpenny Bridge, a steel structure built to replace a wooden and iron one that collapsed in 1877, killing eight people and injuring 60. It was originally a toll bridge, charging a toll of one half penny per person.

Right: the riverside path leads from Pulteney Weir out to the far west of the city.

KENNET AND AVON CANAL

At the point where the waterways meet, go left on the towpath, which is part of the **Kennet and Avon Canal** ❸ where you can watch narrowboats navigating the locks in Bath. The first lock you see (number seven) has a side pond and pumping station that pumps in water to replace what's lost each time the lock is opened. The second (eight/nine) has a chamber with a depth of 19ft 5in (6m), making it Britain's second-deepest canal lock. The canal, which celebrated its 200th anniversary in 2010, was a major achievement in its day, allowing goods to be transported to London and Bristol in just four days. The canal had enjoyed just over 25 years' return on its significant investment before the age of the train, which signalled doom for the canal. In the 1960s, the Kennet and Avon Canal Trust was formed to help save the neglected waterway. Restoration involved a collaboration between staff from British Waterways and volunteer labour. Rebuilding was a long process but in 1990, it was finally reopened to through traffic from Bath to Reading and is now navigable by narrowboats and other craft while the towpath is popular with walkers and cyclists.

PRIOR PARK BUILDINGS

Take the path up to road level before lock 8/9, emerging into the Bath 'village' of Widcombe, next to the Baptist Church, with its biblical texts painted on the roof, 'You must be born again' and 'Prepare to meet your God', which are visible as you arrive in the city by train from London. The texts first appeared in 1903. Turn right and head for the pedestrian crossing, walk across Claverton Street and go left a short distance before turning right on Prior Park Road, following signs for Prior Park. The White Hart pub *(see p.67)*, on the left with its distinctive deer over the door, was built for the stonemasons working and living nearby. A plaque on the homes on the right states that they were built for the workers at Ralph Allen's stone quarries.

At the end of the row of cottages, walk up the cobbled street at Prior Park

⑤ Widcombe Manor

Widcombe Manor, on Church Street, is one of Bath's grandest homes. Built in 1656, it was remodelled in 1727 for local MP Philip Bennet. Henry Fielding lived in the mansion's lodge while writing *Tom Jones*. From 1955, it was home to entrepreneur and inventor Jeremy Fry and was infamous for its wild parties with guests such as the late Princess Margaret and Anthony Armstrong-Jones, who were frequent visitors. It is now a private house.

Above: Prior Park, one of the finest Palladian mansions in Britain, sits within beautifully landscaped gardens overlooking the city.

Ⓥ Bath Skyline Walk

A swathe of land above Bath is owned by the National Trust, which has established a 6-mile (10km) circular walk around the city. It offers breathtaking views of Bath's skyline and the surrounding countryside, and encompasses tranquil woodlands, hidden valleys, meadows filled with wild flowers, an Iron Age hill-fort, Roman settlements, and Sham Castle, commissioned in 1762 by Ralph Allen to 'improve the prospect' from his town house. The Skyline walk is the Trust's most frequently downloaded walking trail.

Above: Sham Castle.

cottages and take an immediate left to admire the brook and the splendid terrace, **Prior Park Buildings ❹**, with its central pedimented section. Walk on past the garden centre on the right, which has a good café *(see p.67)* if you need a break before climbing the hill. Lyncombe Vale, further up to the right, is a peaceful road with a raised pavement supporting a stream where Jane Austen used to enjoy walking. Though this area cannot match the splendour of the grandest parts of Georgian Bath, it has the finest views, most peaceful walks and greatest variety of scenery.

BATH ABBEY CEMETERY

Before crossing to the other side of the road, it's worth a peek inside **Bath Abbey Cemetery ❺**, one of the city's overlooked jewels. It has been cleaned up in recent years while still maintaining its status as a wildlife haven. A tombstone trail leaflet is available for sale at the garden centre. Among the gravestones is a monument to Bathonians killed in the Crimean War and a memorial to the actor and playwright Arnold Ridley,

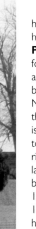

his quarries at the top of the hill to his wharf on the river at the bottom. **Prior Park** 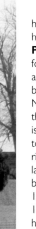, which has parking only for the disabled, encourages visitors to arrive on foot, by taxi, via the open-top bus tour or on public transport, on the No. 1 bus from Dorchester St, near the bus station *(see p.119)*. Prior Park is now a private school and is not open to the public, but the building's exterior can still be admired from the lovely landscaped grounds, which are owned by the National Trust (Apr–Oct daily 10.30am–5.30pm, Nov–Mar Sat–Sun 10am–5.30pm; charge). The country home of Ralph Allen *(see p.8–9)*, the mansion was built by John Wood the Elder between 1734 and 1742 close to Allen's stone quarries. With its imposing portico supported by giant Corinthian columns, this is rated as one of the finest Palladian buildings in Britain. It was, in its way, the first show home, built to demonstrate the beauty and versatility of the stone from Allen's quarry. Philip Thicknesse, a prominent member of Bath society at the time, described it as 'a noble seat, which sees all Bath and which was built, probably, for all Bath to see'. The advertising worked, as the stone was widely adopted in Bath and can be seen on

who played Private Godfrey in the beloved BBC sitcom *Dad's Army*. It's a beautiful, peaceful spot with some fine views of the city. Entry is free and the cemetery is open at all times.

PRIOR PARK

At the cemetery entrance, cross over carefully and prepare for an increasingly steep climb up the hill for about half a mile. It was along this stretch that Allen built a tramway with wagons on tracks, one of the earliest uses of a rail system, to convey the Bath stone from

---

Ⓕ The American Museum

The only museum of Americana outside the US, the American Museum (Claverton House; tel: 01225 460503; Tue–Sun late Mar–Oct noon–5pm, late Nov–22 Dec until 4.30pm; charge) houses a series of re-created rooms, as well as the best collection of quilts outside the US. There's also plenty to entertain children. The house, to the southeast of Bath, has a rich history: Britain's wartime leader Winston Churchill made his first political speech here when he was 23.

Above: sundial outside the museum.

Above: the beautiful landscaped grounds of Prior Park offer one of the most spectacular views of the city.

many other notable buildings in the country, including Buckingham Palace.

Garden Seat

It was at Prior Park that Allen held open house to the leading statesmen, writers and artists of the day, such as William Pitt, Alexander Pope, Henry Fielding and Thomas Gainsborough. The munificent Squire Allworthy in Fielding's *Tom Jones* was based on Allen. The mansion has twice succumbed to devastating fires, the first in 1836. The building was gutted again in 1991, when flames and smoke billowing from the central block of the building could be seen across the city. The building was restored both times.

The delightful walk through the 28-acre (11-hectare) landscape gar-

---

Ⓕ The Natural Theatre Company

At the bottom of Widcombe Hill is the distinctive headquarters of the Natural Theatre Company, with carvings outside of some of the troupe's most distinctive characters. The internationally renowned company has played on all five continents in 66 countries, with its unique brand of unusual and accessible theatre. The company, led by co-founder Ralph Oswick (whose alter ego Lady Margaret had her own Radio 4 show), is much loved in Bath and is part of the city's cultural fabric.

Above: the Naturals take their surreal humour to the streets once more.

den, which has undergone significant restoration work in recent years to return it as far as possible to its original condition, takes in splendid views of Bath with the highlight being a Palladian bridge, one of only four in the world. If you take a close look at the bridge, you can see graffiti carved into the stone, some of it dating from the late 18th century. The grounds, which were designed by the famous landscape gardener Lancelot 'Capability' Brown and the poet Alexander Pope, also include a lake, an ice house, a summer house, reconstructed in 2004 from a photograph of 1912. There is an on-going programme of events, including outdoor theatre, both for adults and children, family activities, trails and a variety of wildlife to spot.

From Prior Park, you can return to the city centre via the same route, content in the knowledge that it's downhill all the way.

E Eating Out

Hon Fusion
25 Claverton Buildings; tel: 01225 446020; www.honfusion.com; daily noon–11pm.
Hon Fusion is always busy and offers an authentic Chinese dining experience. It has a delicious selection of dishes, from Szechuan-style chicken to green vegetables in oyster sauce. Very popular, especially with the local Chinese community. Dim sum at lunch time. £–££

Kindling Coffee Co
9A Claverton Buildings; tel: 01225 442125; Mon–Fri 8am–4.30pm, Sat–Sun 9am–3pm.
This well-liked independently run café serves organic and Fairtrade brews and herbal teas, along with sandwiches, bacon baps and sausage rolls, sweet pastries, rolls and cakes. There's a no-frills interior with a few seats outside and Wi-fi access. £

Ring of Bells
10 Widcombe Parade; tel: 01225 448870; www.ringobellswidcombe. co.uk; Mon–Fri lunch and dinner, Sat–Sun noon–late.
A bustling gastro-pub with scrubbed wooden tables and benches. The menu contains dishes such as sea bass with mussels or roast lamb with Madeira sauce. Helpful staff. Sunday is music night. A good alternative if the nearby White Hart is full. ££

Riverside Café
17 Argyle Street; tel: 01225 480532; www.riversidecafebath.co.uk; daily breakfast, lunch and (from Mar–Oct) dinner.
This small restaurant has a lovely location, tucked away in the arch of Pulteney Bridge, offering outdoor seating with its views of the spectacular weir and the River Avon. Great for people-watching. The food is straightforward and traditional, with fish and chips, pasta, veggie burgers and a range of ciabatta sandwiches. £–££

Secret Garden Café
Prior Park Road; tel: 01225 789788; www.cafesecretgarden.co.uk; Mon–Sat 8.30am–5pm, Sun 10am–4pm.
Located in Prior Park Garden Centre, this café is a popular spot for breakfast, lunch or afternoon cream tea. Good for vegetarians but carnivores are not forgotten with some excellent homemade burgers on the menu. The coffee is first-class, too. £

White Hart
Widcombe Parade; tel: 01225 313985; www.whitehartbath.co.uk; daily lunch, Mon–Sat dinner.
One of Bath's best gastro-pubs, it fills up quickly so book ahead if you can. The unpretentious but inspired menu features dishes such as confit of duck with puy lentils, or rib-eye steak with tarragon mustard butter, and the best French fries in town. Service is always friendly. Relaxed and informal with great ales, a good wine selection and a pleasant beer garden. ££

Tour 6

Bath and the Countryside in Film

This 40-mile (64km), full-day driving tour takes in historic villages and country homes that have been the backdrop to some magical films, including the Harry Potter series

Bath, with its elegant Georgian terraces and sweeping crescents, has been the ideal backdrop for many Jane Austen adaptations and scores of other period dramas. Due to its popularity with film-makers, Bath has a council-run Film Office to promote film-making in the area and to assist producers.

HOLLYWOOD TO BOLLYWOOD

You will need a car for the countryside section of the trip, but you can start by visiting prominent locations in the centre of **Bath ❶** or you can tick these off while doing other tours in this guide. You can start, for example, at the Pump Room, whose graceful

Highlights

- Lacock
- Castle Combe
- Bowood House
- Dyrham Park

18th-century setting has featured in the 1994 and 2006 adaptations of Jane Austen's *Persuasion*, and *The Music Lovers* (1969), a film about the Russian composer Tchaikovsky, directed by Ken Russell with screenplay by Melvyn Bragg, which the Pump Room was passed off as the Moscow conservatoire. The elegant room was also seen in the 2008 BBC television programme

F Film Tours

The Bath Film Office has created a map detailing film and TV productions made in the area, available from the Tourist Information Centre or from the Bath Tourism Plus website (www.visitbath.co.uk). Key sights featured include the Royal Crescent, the Circus, the Assembly Rooms and the Pump Room, as well as many locations in the surrounding countryside. If you're part of a large group, you can also arrange your own guided walks of Bath's cinematic history through Clapperboard Tours (www.clapperboardtours.co.uk).

Left and Above: the Assembly Rooms were the setting for scenes in the film *The Duchess* starring Keira Knightley.

Bonekickers, a bonkers and short-lived drama about a team of Bath-based mystery-solving archaeologists.

The Roman Baths next door featured in the 1976 adaptation of *Joseph Andrews*, based on Henry Fielding's picaresque tale of a naive 18th-century footman. Not far away, the 2006 BBC version of Bram Stoker's classic tale *Dracula* starring David Suchet was filmed in Abbey Green and North Parade Buildings.

The legendary director Stanley Kubrick filmed parts of *Barry Lyndon* (1975), his epic version of Thackeray's story about a rogue's rise and fall in 18th-century society, in Royal Victoria Park and, outside Bath, at Corsham Court and Longleat *(see p.99)*. More recently, the hugely successful *Les Misérables* (2012) made dramatic use of Pulteney Weir *(see box p.46)*.

It's not been all literary adaptations, though. The 1963 film, *80,000 Suspects*, focused on a smallpox epidemic threatening the city, while the 2006 Bollywood extravaganza *Cheeni Kum*

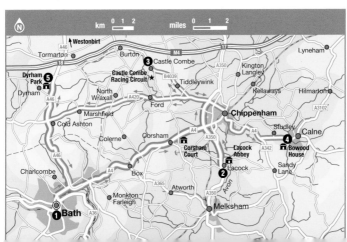

Above: Lacock village has provided a backdrop for numerous films and TV dramas.

(Sugarless) was shot in Grand Parade, Orange Grove, Great Pulteney Street and Prior Park.

PERIOD LIVING

Other films and TV series to have made use of Bath include the BBC's 1987 adaptation of Jane Austen's *Northanger Abbey* (Assembly Rooms, No. 1 Royal Crescent and the Abbey); *The Duchess* (2008) starring Keira Knightley as the scandalous 18th-century aristocrat the Duchess of Devonshire (Assembly Rooms, Royal Crescent and the Holburne Museum); the Inspector Morse episode *Death is Now My Neighbour* (1997); the long-running BBC drama *Casualty*; and the 2003 version of *Vanity Fair* with Reese Witherspoon (Sydney Place, Beauford Square, Holburne Museum and Great Pulteney Street).

STAR CITY

Film figures who live or once lived in and around Bath include the Holly-wood superstar Nicolas Cage, who had a home in the Circus as well as Midford Castle outside Bath. The *Monty Python* and *Fawlty Towers* star

John Cleese who moved to Bath in 2010, while film director Ken Loach (*Kes* and the 2006 Palme d'Or winner *The Wind that Shakes the Barley*) is a long-time resident and supporter of Bath City football club. He brought ac-tor and football legend Eric Cantona to the club while promoting their 2009 collaboration *Looking for Eric*. Other film figures with Bath links include pro-ducer/director Stephen Woolley (*Absolute Beginners* and *The Crying Game*); actor Anthony Head (*Buffy the Vampire Slayer*, *Little Britain* and *Merlin*); and husband-and-wife thespians Timothy West and Prunella Scales.

LACOCK

For the next part of the tour, you will need a car to see some of Britain's most beautiful historic villages, which have served as a backdrop for numer-ous classic films. At the picture-post-card village of **Lacock ❷**, you can walk in the footsteps of the stars of Harry Potter. The village was also fea-tured in the BBC drama *The Cranford Chronicles*, adaptations of *Emma*, *The Mayor of Casterbridge* and *Moll Flan-ders*, the classic 1995 version of Jane

Harry Potter and the Historic Abbey

Start at **Lacock Abbey** (01249 730459; Feb–Oct daily 11am–5.30pm, Nov–Jan Sat–Sun 11am–4pm, Abbey rooms closed Tue all year; charge), used as a location for three of the Harry Potter films and *The Other Boleyn Girl* (2008) starring Scarlett Johansson and Natalie Portman. The abbey's Chapter House and Warming Room were used as stand-ins for classrooms at Hogwarts in *Philosopher's Stone* and *Chamber of Secrets*. The Warming Room houses a cauldron, which looks like it could have been one of the props, but is actually an original from 1500. Other scenes set at Hogwarts were filmed in the magnificent medieval cloisters, while some of the impressive statues in the abbey's grand hall have a distinct Potteresque feel. The 2013 fantasy adventure film

Austen's *Pride and Prejudice* with Colin Firth as Mr Darcy, and *The Wolfman* (2010), starring Oscar-winner Benicio del Toro as the lycanthrope.

From Bath, the 14-mile (22km) journey should take just over 30 minutes. Head east on the A4 towards Chippenham and London. Off the A4 is the historic home **Corsham Court**, where Stanley Kubrick shot his 1975 film *Barry Lyndon*, and you should also be able to glimpse the entrance to Box tunnel. When the 2-mile (3.2km) railway tunnel was opened by Brunel in 1841, it was then the longest tunnel in the world and sceptical MPs feared the public would be too scared to use it. The house was also used for the Merchant Ivory film *Remains of the Day* (1993). About 12 miles (19km) outside Bath, head south on the A350, which will be signposted for Lacock. Keep following these signs to this delightfully unspoilt village and pull in to the large car park on the right close to the centre. The enchanting National Trust-owned village's immediate appeal lies not only in its quaint architecture, but in its lack of telegraph wires, poles and road markings, which has made it a natural film location.

F Cinema Pioneer

Bath played a role in the birth of film, through cinema pioneer William Friese-Green (1855–1921), a photographer with a studio at 23 Gay Street and later at 9 The Corridor. Friese-Green's partnership with Bath native John Rudge paved the way for the first film camera. A bronze tablet in New Bond Street Place marks their contribution.

Above: William Friese-Green and his son Claude, *c*.1908.

Above: Lacock Abbey doubled up as Hogwarts in the Harry Potter films.

Mariah Mundi and the Midas Box, starring Michael Sheen, was also filmed in the abbey.

The Abbey's Habits

The abbey is an intriguing mix of medieval, Renaissance and Gothic architecture. It was founded in 1232 as a nunnery, but following the Dissolution of the Monasteries, in 1539, Henry VIII pensioned off the nuns and sold the property to William Sharrington, who set about converting it into a home, retaining many of the abbey's original features. You can visit many of the rooms, including the recently opened wine cellar. The abbey was once owned by one of the pioneers of photography, William Henry Fox Talbot *(see box, opposite)*.

Lacock Village

You can wander around the village, taking in the beautiful lime-washed and half-timbered stone buildings, some dating from the 13th century but mostly from the 17th and 18th centuries. The oldest building (1206) is King John's Hunting Lodge tearooms. Look out for the 18th-century lock-up where drunks and others were forced to spend the night. Drop in to Lacock Bakery, which has food made on the premises and staff dressed in traditional costumes like characters from Cranford.

In fact, wandering the streets, you could easily imagine yourself in some period drama, although the effect is somewhat spoilt by residents' cars parked outside their homes. In *Harry Potter and the Half-Blood Prince* the village became Budleigh Babberton,

---

Ⓖ Westonbirt

If you want to see English nature at its best, it's worth taking the 20-mile (32km) trip out of Bath to the wonderful national arboretum at Westonbirt in the south Cotswolds (www.forestry.gov.uk/westonbirt). Amid 600 acres (243 hectares) of picturesque landscape, there are 17 miles (28km) of paths and 16,000 trees, including some of the oldest, rarest and largest in the UK. It's worth seeing at any time of the year but is particularly stunning in the autumn.

where Harry and Dumbledore go to visit Professor Horace Slughorn.

CASTLE COMBE

From Lacock, you can visit **Castle Combe** ❸, widely regarded as one of Britain's prettiest villages, which also has a rich cinematic history. Return to the A350 and head north. After a few miles, go east on the A420 signed for Bristol and then follow signs for the racing circuit at Castle Combe. You travel through the small village of Tiddleywink and a Cotswold Area of Outstanding Natural Beauty. After passing the circuit on the left, where members of the public can experience knuckle car rides and track days in cars or on motorbikes (www.castle combecircuit.co.uk), follow the signs to Castle Combe, an archetypal Cotswold village, much visited by tourists but retaining most of its charm. You have to park in the large free car park outside the village as Castle Combe has parking restrictions. You can park in the village if you're visiting one of the pubs and can find a space, otherwise you need to walk about half a mile along the road from the car park (be careful as there is no pavement for much of the way).

Dr Dolittle

The lovely village, with a population of just 350, will be familiar to fans of the 1967 film *Dr Dolittle*, a musical in which Rex Harrison could famously 'talk to the animals'. The first house you see on the left on entering Castle Combe from the car park is the Dower House, a yellow building that was Dr Dolittle's house in the film. The film-makers spent three months on location here, somehow transforming the landlocked village into the fictitious seaport of Puddleby on Sea. The small bridge over the river was used to portray a sea wall with boats bobbing in the gentle waters. Other films made here include *Stardust* (2006) with Michelle Pfeiffer, Robert De Niro and Sienna Miller, and, in 2010, Steven Spielberg's version of the Michael Morpurgo novel and stage play *War Horse*.

Castle Combe is a typical example of a Saxon street village, with most of the buildings dating from the 14th century including the Market Cross at its heart. There is a 13th-century church, St Andrew's, and there was a castle here in Norman times, but now only the raised earthworks remain to mark its location.

⑤ Photography Pioneer

William Henry Fox Talbot, who lived in Lacock Abbey in the 1900s, had a keen interest in the sciences and was a key figure in the development of photography. His negative of an oriel window in Lacock's South Gallery is the oldest in existence. In the abbey's barn, the Fox Talbot Museum of Photography celebrates his achievements and examines the history of the art form. It also features a display of cameras through the years and temporary exhibitions.

Above: Fox Talbot at work at his studio in Reading, c.1845.

Above: Castle Combe became Puddleby on Sea in the film *Dr Dolittle*.

BOWOOD HOUSE

A short detour takes you to another grand house that's been used in films. **Bowood House ④** (house: daily late Mar–early Nov 11am–5.30pm, grounds 11am–6pm, until 4pm in autumn; charge) is 2½ miles (4km) off the A4, a few miles east of Chippenham. The Palladian home of the Earl and Countess of Shelburne, it offers a fine interior, including the laboratory where Dr Joseph Priestley discovered oxygen. The home was featured in the BBC's 1986 version of Austen's *Northanger Abbey*. There's a well-designed adventure playground for pre-teen children, a superb pirate ship made by a former boat-builder and an indoor soft play area. Opened in 2013, Tractor Ted's Little Farm, a farm-themed play park, is popular with young children.

The grounds of Bowood are suitably grand, and especially delightful in spring when the rhododendrons and azaleas bloom (the rhododendron park is open during the flowering season from mid-April to early June). The long lake below the terraces was created by landscape gardener Lancelot 'Capability' Brown in the 1760s.

DYRHAM PARK

The last of the grand houses on this tour is **Dyrham Park ⑤**, 8 miles (13km) from Bath. From Castle Combe, follow the A420 west until it meets the A46 and then head north, away from Bath, to Dyrham (special buses to Dyrham also depart from Bath Bus Station). Dyrham Park (house: mid-Mar–Oct Fri–Tue 11am–5pm, daily in July and Aug; grounds: year-round 11am–5.30pm; charge) is a beautiful mansion with formal gardens and a deer park, which have featured in a number of films, including *Persua-*

Above: deer at Dyrham Park.

sion (2002) and *Sense and Sensibility* (2007). It figured prominently in *The Remains of the Day* (1993), with Anthony Hopkins as the dedicated butler putting duty above his love for Emma Thompson. An aerial view of Dyrham was also used in the 2008 blockbuster *Australia* with Nicole Kidman.

The house, dating from 1692–1704, has lavish Dutch collections in the showrooms, and you can get a feel for what life would have been like for Hopkins' butler and others in the servants' quarters, where there are lots of hands-on activities. There's a play area for children, but the highlight for them is the wild and hilly parkland in front of the house and the chance to see deer roaming around the estate. The deer park has existed here for centuries (deor hamm being Anglo-Saxon for deer enclosure).

Return to Bath, heading south on the A46, then west on the A4.

Ⓔ Eating Out

Bell Inn
The Wharf, Bowden Hill, Lacock; tel: 01249 730308; www.thebellatlacock. co.uk; daily lunch and dinner.
Located just outside the village, the Bell is a quieter option for a meal or drink. Renowned for its first-class ales and ciders and home-cooked food, the menu ranges from classic pub comfort dishes and lunchtime platters to succulent locally-sourced steaks and medallions of pork. ££

Castle Inn Hotel
Castle Combe; tel: 01249 783030; www.castle-inn.info; daily lunch and dinner.
Next to the Market Cross, this hotel and pub retains many of its original features dating from the Middle Ages. You can choose from a traditional bar menu for light lunches or a more sophisicated à la carte menu. ££

King John's Hunting Lodge
Church Street, Lacock; tel: 01249 730313; http://kingjohnslodge.2day. ws; Feb–mid-Dec Wed–Sun 10.30am–5pm.
The oldest building in Lacock (with parts dating from the early 13th century), this historic venue serves light lunches and cream teas. The main part still has much of the original cruck beam structure, whilst the rear of the building was added to in Tudor times. There's a log fire in winter and a lovely garden in the summer. On the menu are crumpets,

cheese muffins, scones and other home-made cakes and pastries. £–££

Bybrook Restaurant
Manor House Hotel, Castle Combe; tel: 01249 782206; www.manorhouse. co.uk; Tue–Sun lunch, daily dinner.
This prestigious restaurant has retained its Michelin star gained in 2009. The menu includes dishes such as ravioli of Salcombe Bay crab and slow cooked rump of Wiltshire lamb with cauliflower couscous. For a more casual meal, try the Clubhouse, which is open to non-members. £££

Salutation Inn
The Gibb, Castle Combe; tel: 01249 783014; www.thesalutationinn. co.uk; Tue–Sat lunch and dinner, Sun noon–5pm.
Nestled in the hamlet of The Gibb, close to Castle Combe, this 17th-century pub is rapidly gaining a name for great hospitality and good food. Expect the likes of lemon sole with baby chard, mouth-watering steaks and super Sunday roasts. ££

The Sign of the Angel
Church Street, Lacock; tel: 01249 730230; www.lacock.co.uk. Tue–Sun lunch and dinner, Mon dinner only.
An atmospheric building with original beams and floorboards and a pleasant beer garden. The impressive food includes seared scallops with black pudding and bacon, and roasted duck breast with spiced red cabbage. Log fires in winter. ££–£££

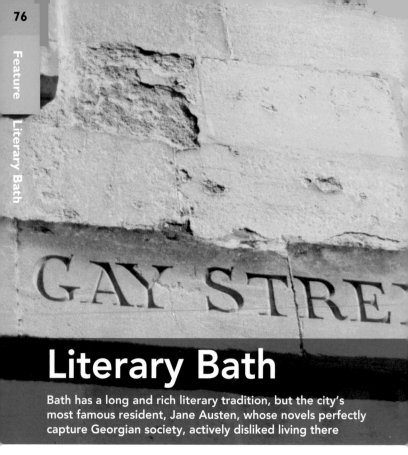

Literary Bath

Bath has a long and rich literary tradition, but the city's most famous resident, Jane Austen, whose novels perfectly capture Georgian society, actively disliked living there

NO FAN OF BATH

Jane Austen (1775–1817) is the true star of Bath's literary firmament but she was far from its biggest fan. In her novels, she often portrays Bath as a tiresome, petty city that is only good for gossip, parties and balls. Having departed for good, she wrote: 'It will be two years tomorrow since we left Bath, with happy feelings of escape!'

In *Northanger Abbey*, one of her characters reflects Austen's views: 'I get so immoderately sick of Bath … though it is vastly well to be here for a few weeks, we would not live here

for millions'. Large parts of *Persuasion* and *Northanger Abbey* are set in the city, giving an insight into the life Austen led in Bath from 1799 to 1806. She stayed in four houses, living at 4 Sydney Place, 13 Queen Square, 27 Green Park Buildings and 25 Gay Street. The writer's association with the city is celebrated at the Jane Austen Centre (see p.27).

DICKENS AND OTHER GREATS

Other writers with Bath connections include novelists Charles Dickens, Samuel Richardson, Henry Fielding

irons'. Dickens often stayed at 35 St James's Square, where he conceived the character of Little Nell from *The Old Curiosity Shop*.

Henry Fielding (1707–54), best known for the comic novel *Tom Jones* (1749), lived in the city along with his sister Sarah, a fellow novelist and a pioneer of children's literature. Fielding based the character of Squire Allworthy in *Tom Jones* on Ralph Allen *(see p.8)*, one of Bath's most famous figures. Fielding was a frequent guest at Allen's mansion Prior Park *(see p.64)*, as was one of his rivals Samuel Richardson (1689–1761), who wrote part of his most celebrated novels *Clarissa* (1748) and *Pamela* while in Bath. Another guest of Allen's was Alexander Pope, the poet whose most famous lines include 'To err is human, to forgive divine' and 'Fools rush in where angels fear to tread'.

The poet Percy Bysshe Shelley (1792–1822) was staying at 5 Abbey Churchyard in 1816 when he learnt that his estranged wife Harriet had been drowned in the Serpentine. A fortnight later, he married Mary Godwin, who at the time was putting the finishing touches to her novel *Frankenstein* (1818) in the city.

Richard Brinsley Sheridan (1751–1816), the playwright who lived at 9 New King Street, fought a ferocious duel in Bath that left him seriously wounded. He is best known for *The School for Scandal*, *The Critic* and *The Rivals* (set in 18th-century Bath).

and his sister Sarah, playwright Richard Brinsley Sheridan, and poets Percy Shelley and Alexander Pope.

Dickens (1812–70) was a frequent visitor and set much of *Pickwick Papers* in Bath, brilliantly satirising the social life, including a scene where Mr Pickwick takes the waters. His servant Sam Weller (also the name of a Bath pub) describes the water as 'having a wery [*sic*] strong flavour o' warm flat

More recent writers with links to Bath include the children's author Jacqueline Wilson, who was born there, the humorist Miles Kington, who lived in nearby Limpley Stoke, Sir Simon Jenkins, former editor of *The Times*, and author Morag Joss, who sets her crime novels in the genteel city. Paul Emmanuelli's *Avon Street – A Tale of Murder in Victorian Bath* (2012) exposes a darker side of Bath's past.

Above: Jane Austen stayed at several locations in the city, including Gay Street.
Top Right: novelist Samuel Richardson.
Bottom Right: an illustration from Henry Fielding's *Tom Jones*.

Tour 7

Bristol

Though not as postcard pretty as Bath, Bristol has a number of attractions that are worth seeking out. This 1-mile (2km) tour can be done as a day-trip from Bath

While Bath was primarily a city of pleasure, Bristol, 13 miles (21km) away, was largely a city of industry. A major British port for 300 years, second only to London, Bristol was – and still is to a lesser extent – the West Country's window on the world and its main magnet for labour. Important since Saxon times, Bristol has a rich history plus an attractive setting. With seagulls wheeling overhead and salty breezes off the Bristol Channel, the city makes an invigorating change from cosy, compact Bath. In more recent years, the area around the floating harbour, near the SS *Great Britain*, has blossomed with a quirky modern bridge, lively arts centres, bars, restaurants and a wide range of visitor attractions.

Highlights

- At-Bristol
- Bristol Aquarium
- SS *Great Britain*
- John Cabot's Ship
- Bristol Cathedral
- Bristol Zoo

GETTING THERE

The best way to get to Bristol on public transport is by rail. Regular trains leave from Bath Spa to Bristol Temple Meads (journey time about 15 minutes). You can walk to the centre from there, take a bus or use one of the ferry boats. There are two direct roads to Bristol from Bath, the A4 and the A431 (the lat-

should follow signposts to The Centre Promenade).

From the railway station, you can follow signposts to the Harbourside (a 15- to 20-minute walk, or take bus Nos 8 or 9), the focus of a cluster of attractions and museums that have flowered in the redeveloped docks, including the **Arnolfini** arts centre (Narrow Quay; tel: 0117 917 2300; www.arnolfini. org.uk; Tues–Sun 11am–6pm; free). The Arnolfini is one of the country's leading centres for contemporary arts, with galleries, a trendy café-bar, and arthouse cinema in a skilfully converted 1830s tea warehouse overlooking the floating harbour.

Left: the At-Bristol interactive science centre. **Above**: art at the Arnolfini.

ter passing Avon Valley Railway for steam train rides at Bitton). Buses to Bristol (journey time around 45 minutes) leave from Bath Bus Station in Dorchester Street every 30 minutes (Bristol Bus Station is located in Marlborough Street near Broadmead Shopping Centre, from where you

AT-BRISTOL

Nearby is **At-Bristol ❶** (Anchor Road; tel: 0845 345 1235; www.at-bristol.org.uk; Mon–Fri 10am–5pm, Sat–Sun and school holidays 10am–6pm; charge). One of the UK's biggest interactive science centres, this is a great place for the whole family. There are more than 300 hands-on exhibits, live science shows, workshops, a Planetarium, experiments you

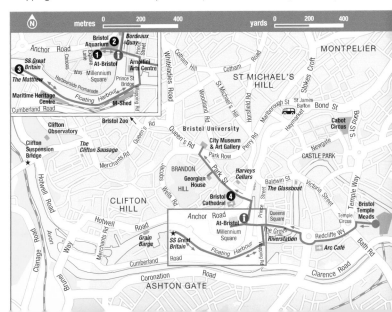

can get stuck into, meet-the-expert sessions, and a studio where you can create your own TV shows or become an animator for a day, inspired by the Bristol-based Aardman studios, the multi-Oscar winning team behind Wallace and Gromit and other beloved characters, including the mischievous Morph. The museum is spread over several floors and there's plenty to keep you entertained, including the strangely addictive virtual volleyball, a chance to be involved in the construction of a huge Lego house, a tornado you can walk through, and All About Us, an interactive exhibition revealing the mysteries of the human body, including a real human brain exhibit. Learn about waste and recycling, take a sporting challenge, make and launch your own flying object or just investigate how things work.

UNDER THE SEA

Next to At-Bristol, at the £4m **Bristol Aquarium ❷** (Anchor Road; tel: 0117 929 8929; www.bristolaquarium. co.uk; daily 10am–5pm, last entry 4pm; charge), more than 40 habitats, playing host to 7,000 fish from 750 different species, take you on a journey from the British coast, through warmer waters and tropical rainforests to exotic coral seas. On the way, you get to have close encounters with sharks, stingrays, sea horses, giant octopus, and shoals of colourful fish. The aquarium is imaginatively presented with an underwater tunnel of reinforced glass, where you can literally come face to face with all manner of marine life. In a 300,000-litre tank you can see a shipwreck display, complete with sharks and rays. There are also daily talks, feeding displays and a Learning Lab for children.

FLOATING HARBOUR

Just outside At-Bristol at 1 Canons Road, you'll find the Tourist Information Centre (tel: 0906 711 2191; www. visitbristol.co.uk; Sun–Fri 11am–4pm, Sat 10am–4pm). Also here is a small statue of Hollywood legend Cary Grant, known simply as Archibald Leach when he left his native Bristol. There are numerous cafés, bars and restaurants nearby, particularly along the Watershed, a finger of the floating harbour, created in 1810 as a non-tidal dock and now one of the city's most

Below: the SS *Great Britain* transported goods and people for nearly a century.

Above: luggage hold, SS *Great Britain*.

vibrant areas. From below Neptune's statue on the Watershed, ferries leave for the SS *Great Britain* and to other landing stages every 40 minutes or so. Alternatively, the ship can be reached by walking along Narrow Quay, past the Arnolfini, and across Prince Street Bridge, where a right turn leads along the south side of the floating harbour. On the way, you'll see a statue of John Cabot, the explorer who set off from Bristol in 1497 to discover Newfoundland, the tracks of the old steam railway on the docks and a series of designer apartments.

SS *GREAT BRITAIN*

The **SS *Great Britain*** ❸ (www.ss greatbritain.org; daily Mar–Oct 10am–5.30pm, Nov–Mar 10am–4.30pm; charge) represents Bristol's heyday as a major shipbuilding centre, when the city inspired the expression 'shipshape and Bristol fashion'. It's worth a visit to Bristol for this wonderful attraction alone, which celebrates the world's first great ocean liner. It's easy to understand why the museum has collected numerous accolades over the years, including a silver medal

from South West Tourism's Excellence Awards for Large Visitor Attraction of the year (2011/12) and three Michelin stars in the Michelin Guide to Great Britian (2012).

There's a lot to keep the whole family entertained at this all-weather attraction. You start by going underwater to see the outside of the ship as it would have been in the dry dock where it was built, while gazing up at the sea through the glass above you. Get up close to the super-size iron hull, which in 1843 made her the biggest, strongest ship yet built; marvel at a replica of her massive steampowered propeller, an innovative piece of engineering; and explore the holes made in the hull when the ship was scuttled off the Falkland Islands. Head for the dockyard museum to discover the history of this magnificent vessel and the many uses she was put to in her relatively short life. There are hands-on activities to keep children entertained and interesting accounts of the ship's colourful history. The highlight is the tour of the ship itself. Arm yourself with an audioguide, which gives you an insight from the perspective of a first-class or steerage passenger, maritime archaeologist or, for children, Sinbad the

Ⓖ Ferry Boats

The Bristol Ferry Boat Company service is a great way of avoiding Bristol's traffic-clogged streets. If you arrive at Bristol Temple Meads railway station, there's a ferry boat stop nearby that can transport you to the SS *Great Britain* and other sights on the harbourside. The scheduled waterbus service is used by commuters and sightseers alike, so best avoided at rush hour. For prices and timetables, see www.bristolferry.com.

Above: the floating harbour and the Arnolfini Arts Complex.

ship's cat. The audio tours are also available in French and German. You can wander at your leisure experiencing the sights, sounds and smells of life on board, including some nice comic touches. You can see the engine room and galley, compare the first-class quarters (and its opulent dining room) with the cramped conditions in steerage, and check out the medical quarters where an unfortunate passenger is being treated.

Ocean-going history

The SS *Great Britain* was the first propeller-driven iron ocean-going ship in history. Designed by the great Isambard Kingdom Brunel, chief engineer of the Great Western Steamship Company, the vessel measured 322ft (98m) in length, had a gross tonnage of 2,936, and was fitted with six masts for use when the wind was favourable in order to save coal. As well as surpassing other ships in terms of speed and capacity, she set new standards of comfort. By combining size, power and innovative technology, Brunel created a vessel that became the template for all modern ships.

But in 1846, the year after her first voyage, the captain grounded the ship off the Irish coast. The cost of repairs and repeated attempts at refloating bankrupted the Great Western Steamship Company and the ship was bought by Gibbs, Bright and Company of Liverpool. She was substantially altered for her relaunch in 1852, after which she spent 24 years transporting emigrants to Australia. It is estimated that some 250,000 Australians are descended from her passengers. She was later used to carry cargo to San Francisco and was commandeered during the World War I to supply coal to Britain's warships.

Incredible hulk

At the end of her working life, the ship was bought by the Falkland Islands Company when she limped into Port Stanley harbour in 1886 after being badly damaged in a storm. She was

ation. In all, the SS *Great Britain* sailed around the world 32 times, clocking up more than one million miles at sea.

The Dockyard Café Bar has a delightful waterfront terrace and serves reasonable food, or you can picnic in the outdoor Riggers' Yard if the weather is good.

JOHN CABOT'S SHIP

Near the SS *Great Britain* is **The Matthew** (tel: 0117 927 6868; www.matthewbristol.co.uk; charge), a reconstruction of the ship in which John Cabot set sail for America. It was built in 1997 to mark the 500th anniversary of Cabot's voyage, when he discovered Newfoundland, and now provides harbour cruises including a two-hour tour with a fish-and-chip supper or an afternoon cream tea.

used as a storage hulk, a floating warehouse for coal and wool, until 1933 when she became unsafe. She was towed to a secluded bay and scuttled in shallow waters. More than 40 years ago, she was salvaged from the Falkland Islands in a remarkable operation and returned to her home in Bristol, where she has been painstakingly restored to be admired by a new gener-

Return along the quay to M Shed (www.mshed.org; Tue–Fri 10am–5pm, Sat–Sun until 6pm), an innovative museum that aims to tell the story of Bristol. Housed in a 1950s transit shed, it explores the city's history from prehistoric times to the 21st century. Wherever possible, the idea is to let Bristol's people tell their own story. Rich collections of objects, art and

Ⓕ Banksy in Bristol

One of Britain's most popular living artists is also the least recognised. Banksy, who was born in Bristol, keeps his identity secret, but that hasn't stopped his particular brand of street art from gaining a massive following. An impromptu show of his work at Bristol City Museum and Art Gallery in 2009 had queues round the block. You can take a self-guided tour throughout the city to view the artist's most famous works. Details are available from the tourist information office.

Above: satirical street art.

Above: the old harbourside entrance now leads to shops and restaurants.

archives also play an important part in bringing their stories to life. There is an exciting programme of changing exhibitions throughout the year.

BRISTOL CATHEDRAL

If you head back to the Watershed, Park Street leads uphill to the city centre and the university. Halfway up on the left are College Green and **Bristol Cathedral** ❹, originally the church

Ⓥ **Clifton Observatory**

Close to Clifton Suspension Bridge is Clifton Observatory (Apr–Oct 11am–5pm, Nov–Mar noon–4pm; charge), with a camera obscura offering spectacular 360-degree views of the bridge, the gorge, the downs and the city. The camera, which projects panoramic views of the surrounding area on to a white surface inside a darkened room, is housed in a former mill that was rented in 1828 to William West, an artist, for use as his studio.

of an Augustinian abbey founded in around 1140 by Robert Fitzardinge. The abbey was closed following the dissolution of the monasteries in 1539, but the church was reopened as a cathedral in 1542. It is a rare example of a hall church, in which the roof is at the same height throughout the building. This makes it extremely strong. Though Bristol was heavily bombed during World War II, the cathedral escaped relatively lightly.

The original unfinished nave was demolished after the dissolution, resulting in a truncated church right up until the mid-19th century. This nave was added in 1868–77 by George Edmund Street. The Elder Lady Chapel (1220) contains some fine naturalistic carvings of animals, including monkeys, linking it to the stone mason who worked on Wells Cathedral, where similar carvings are found (see p.89). The Choir (1298–1330) has lierne-rib vaulting, the earliest of its kind in England. The Eastern Lady Chapel (1298), behind the High Altar, is interesting for its deep green, blue, red and gold paintwork (partially restored in 1935); medieval cathedrals would have been covered in such colours.

On the south aisle is a chapel to the Newton family. Past here is the entrance to the Chapter House and Cloisters. As you turn towards these, note, on the left, the Saxon stone sculpture (c.1050) depicting the Harrowing of Hell (a just-discernible Christ trampling Satan while comforting a pregnant woman), one of the most important pieces of Saxon sculpture in England.

From the cathedral, Park Street rises to Bristol University and the **City Museum and Art Gallery** (tel: 0117 922 3571; Mon–Fri 10am–5pm, Sat–Sun 10am–6pm; free). This Edwardian Baroque building contains good collections on natural history, geology, archaeology, wildlife, dinosaur fossils, pottery and ceramics, silver and paintings. The Egyptology collection, complete with mummies, is particularly strong, and there's a lovely area for under-7s in the Curiosity Gallery. The first floor contains the Balcony Gallery featuring modern art. The second floor galleries contain British and Euro-

Below: the Eastern Lady Chapel.

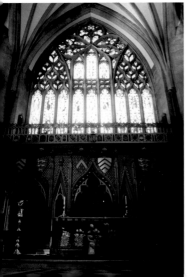

ⓕ St Mary Redcliffe

On the walk into Bristol from Temple Meads station, you pass St Mary Redcliffe Church, built from 1325–75 in the Perpendicular style, characterised by pinnacles and projecting buttresses. Its soaring spire is 285ft (87m) tall. Interesting features of the church include the hexagonal 13th-century north porch with an inner 12th-century porch, fan vaulting and aisled transepts. Queen Elizabeth I described it as the 'fairest, goodliest and most famous parish church in England'.

pean art from 1300, including works from the Bristol School of Artists and a gallery featuring French Impressionist art. In the summer of 2009, the museum hosted an exhibition by Banksy *(see box, p.83)*, the Bristol-born graffiti artist, which saw a surge in visitor numbers. In 2011 he donated his *Angel with Paintpot* sculpture to the museum and it continues to pull in the crowds.

Nearby, on Great George Street is the late 18th-century **Georgian House** (Easter–Oct Wed, Thu, Sat–Sun 10.30am–4pm; July–Aug Tue–Sun 10.30am–4pm; free). Inside, you'll find one of the best-preserved interiors from that time, and it's said to be where Wordsworth first met Coleridge in 1795. Off to the right at the top of Park Street is Park Row and the **Red Lodge** (Apr–Oct Wed, Thur, Sat and Sun 10.30am–4pm, July–Aug Tue–Sun 10.30am–4pm), an Elizabethan house with oak-lined rooms and a Tudor knot garden.

A left turn at the top of Park Street leads into Queen's Road which runs up to Clifton Village (also accessed by buses Nos 8 and 9 from College Green outside the cathedral) where Isambard Kingdom Brunel's **Suspension Bridge**

G Guided Walks

Try a highlights tour (April–Sept Sat; charge, under-12s free), which takes in historic sights and the lively harbourside. To learn more about Bristol's maritime past, join Pete the Pirate for a two-hour tour (Sat–Sun, 2pm; charge). Both tours start from Millennium Square. There are also tours of Brunel's magnificent Clifton Suspension Bridge (April–Oct Sat–Sun 3pm; free), from the tollbooth end. Details from tourist information.

(1829–64) spans the gorge. A Visitor Centre (www.cliftonbridge.org.uk; daily 10am–5pm) relates the story behind the building of the bridge. Brunel never saw the finished bridge, as he died five years before its completion.

BRISTOL ZOO

After visiting the bridge, you may want to wander around Clifton Village, whose Georgian buildings are oc-cupied by interesting shops, and cosy restaurants and cafés. The Royal York Crescent, above the gorge, is the UK's longest (at a quarter of a mile), topping anything in Bath and the rest of Britain. Also, you can visit the nearby **Bristol Zoo Gardens** (www.bristolzoo.org. uk; daily 9am–5.30pm, Oct–Mar until 5pm; charge). Children will enjoy the lemur walk-through, the excellent aerial assault course, Zooropia, and the exciting Explorers' Creek with water play and a chance to hand-feed the lorrikeet parrots. As well as more than 400 exotic and endangered species, there's a butterfly forest and an award-winning seal and penguin area.

SHOPPING

Bristol's shopping experience is not as eclectic as it is in more compact Bath, but it does have a couple of block-buster shopping centres that its smaller cousin can't compete with. **Cabot Circus** (www.cabotcircus.com), is a £500m extension to the otherwise rather mundane Broadmead shopping

Below: Brunel's suspension bridge, a masterpiece of industrial engineering.

centre (www.bristolshoppingquarter.co.uk). The big draw in Cabot Circus is a bijou Harvey Nichols, and there are plenty of other top high-street names and designer stores. Also in the mix in this huge covered mall are restaurants and cafés, a 13-screen cinema and adventure golf. Outside the city centre, the mall at Cribbs Causeway (www.mallcribbs.com) has a large John Lewis department store, 130 big-name stores and 15 cafés and restaurants.

E Eating Out

Arc Café
St Mary Redcliffe Church; tel: 0117 929 1487; http://stmaryredcliffe.co.uk; Tue–Fri 8am–3pm, Sat 10am–3pm. Tucked away in the vaults of this historic church, the Arc is run by staff and volunteers of the Addiction Recovery Agency. Come here for good-value breakfasts, home-cooked lunches, baguettes and scrummy cakes. £

Bordeaux Quay
V-Shed, Canons Way; tel: 0117 943 1200; www.bordeaux-quay.co.uk; Sun–Fri lunch and dinner, Sat dinner only. The first UK restaurant to achieve a gold rating under the Soil Association's sustainable catering scheme. Its European Provincial-style dishes include asparagus, ricotta and parmigiano tartlet and baked Cornish monkfish with parsley risotto. Great location; also houses a brasserie, winebar, deli, cookery school and bakery. ££–£££

The Clifton Sausage
7 Portland Street; tel: 0117 973 1192; www.cliftonsausage.co.uk; Tue–Sun noon–midnight, Mon 6pm–midnight. Perfect for a break from wandering around Clifton, this attractive cosy restaurant packs a meaty punch. But it's not all about sausages, although there are as many as 12 varieties to choose from, there are steaks, poultry and veggie options, too. Comforting desserts to finish. ££

The Glassboat
Welsh Back; tel: 0117 929 0704; www.glassboat.co.uk; Tue–Sat lunch and dinner, Sun brunch 11am–4pm. This boat restaurant, with a glass aft section overlooking the river, is a Bristol institution. The modern British menu includes cod, chorizo and bean stew, and pork belly. Expect romantic, candlelit tables, polished wooden floors and slick service. ££–£££

Grain Barge
Mardyke Wharf, Hotwell Road; tel: 0117 929 9347; www.grainbarge.co.uk; daily lunch and dinner. In a harbourside location, the converted barge is an atmospheric place to eat or just to have a drink. Ethically sourced, well-priced food includes homemade pies, Sunday roasts and more inventive dishes. Eclectic mix of live music on Friday nights. ££

Harveys Cellars
12 Denmark Street; tel: 0117 929 4812; www.harveyscellars.co.uk; Tue–Thur dinner, Fri–Sat lunch, dinner. Housed in medieval cellars, this unique restaurant is centred round a stunning bar, with sherry at its heart. The tempting tapas menu is designed to complement the drink in all its forms. Live music at weekends. ££

Pony and Trap
Newtown, Chew Magna; tel: 01275 332627; www.theponyandtrap.co.uk; Tue–Sun lunch and dinner. Situated 9 miles (14km) south of Bristol, near Chew Magna, this is the only pub in Somerset to have gained a Michelin star. The unpretentious inn boasts a daily-changing menu that is weighty on flavour and committed to using locally sourced ingredients. ££–£££

Riverstation
The Grove; tel: 0117 914 4434; www.riverstation.co.uk; daily lunch, Mon–Sat dinner. A former river-police station, this Mediterranean-influenced restaurant occupies a great location on the waterfront. Brunch at weekends, plus a set-price Sunday lunch. ££

Tour 8

Wells and Glastonbury

Wells Cathedral is a compelling reason to venture out of Bath. You'll need a car for the 40-mile (65km) round trip and it's worth spending at least half a day in Wells

The A367 Wells road is clearly signposted from the south of Bath. Around 10 miles (16km) south of Bath are the market towns of Midsomer Norton and Radstock. In Midsomer Norton, the River Somer runs alongside the main street, making it an attractive place in which to stop for a coffee and browse in the characterful town centre.

From here, the route crosses to the A39, for the descent into **Wells** ❶. Two miles (3km) off to the right, just outside Wells, are **Wookey Hole Caves** (www.wookey.co.uk; daily Apr–Oct 10am–5pm, Nov–Mar 10am–4pm, closed weekdays in Jan; charge) where guided tours explore caves carved out by the River Axe, which rises to the surface inside the

caves. In competition with Cheddar Gorge, Wookey Hole offers other entertainments (many of them rather tacky and mainly aimed at children), including life-size replica dinosaurs, a mirror maze, cave-aged cheese and a pirate-themed golf course. There are also tours of a 19th-century paper mill and demonstrations of paper-making by hand.

Left: the ornate facade of Wells Cathedral. **Above**: Wookey Hole Caves.

F The Wells of Wells

In the tranquil grounds of the Bishop's Palace are the springs that gave Wells its name. They were harnessed by Bishop Beckynton in the 15th century to supply the palace with water and to drive the town's woollen mills. The wells supply 3.4m gallons a day or 40 gallons (182 litres) a second. The Gothic fountain is a late 18th-century replacement for an earlier version.

CATHEDRAL CHURCH OF ST ANDREW

Wells (population: 10,400), 23 miles (37km) from Bath, is effectively a sleepy market town lifted completely out of the ordinary by its stunning **Cathedral Church of St Andrew** and Bishop's Palace. It is the smallest city in England with a cathedral, and small enough to negotiate on foot. Like Bath, it derives its name from natural springs. The Cathedral that you see today was begun in 1179 and completed in 1340. It is in the Early English Gothic style, characterised by pointed arches and ribbed vaulting. Unlike Bath Abbey, it was a cathedral rather than a monastery and survived the Dissolution intact, though it suffered repeated damage during the Civil War and a rebellion in the 17th century.

The exterior

Parking is available in the marketplace, scene of a bustling twice-weekly market (Wed and Sat) and biannual traditional funfairs. There is a tourist information centre here (tel: 01749 671770). From the marketplace, the Penniless Porch – a towered gatehouse where those seeking alms used to congregate in medieval times – leads to the intricately carved West Front, containing one of the largest galleries of medieval sculpture in the world. It is an illustration in stone of the Christian faith, incorporating 293 statues of angels, kings, knights, bishops and saints (13th century) rising to a central band of 12 Apostles (15th century) and the figure of Christ in Majesty at its apex, carved in 1985 by David Wynne to replace the crumbling original. Erosion and destruction by puritans in the 17th century have left many of the lower niches vacant, but the front remains a breathtaking sight, its unusual breadth due to the towers being placed either side of the nave instead of head on. Originally

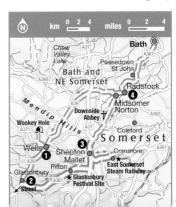

the statues would have numbered around 400 and been richly painted in rather lurid colours.

The interior

Inside the cathedral (daily, evensong Mon–Sat 5.15pm, Sun 3pm; voluntary donation), the eye is swept along the nave to the unique scissor arches. This simple but stunning design is often mistaken as strikingly modern but, built between 1338 and 1348, it was a medieval solution to the problem of sinking tower foundations, and the arches have become a hallmark of the cathedral. In the Middle Ages, the only seating in the cathedral would have been stone benches running around the sides of the naves and their aisles.

To enjoy the splendours of the cathedral, follow this anticlockwise walk, starting at the Sugar Chantry (1489), which commemorates Hugh Sugar, the cathedral's treasurer. Chantries were built by wealthy members of the congregation so that Masses might be offered in their memory after death.

The base of the font was brought from the old Saxon cathedral (on the site of the cloisters); the exquisite 17th-century cover was painted and

Above: the Choir in Wells Cathedral.

gilded in 1982. It's worth lingering over the brilliant carvings on the pillars near the font, which depict scenes from everyday life in the Middle Ages, such as a man taking a thorn out of his foot, a cobbler at work and a man nursing a toothache. The scenes decorating one pillar, carved in around 1190, tell the complete story of a man and a boy stealing fruit from an orchard and being caught, chased and punished by the farmer.

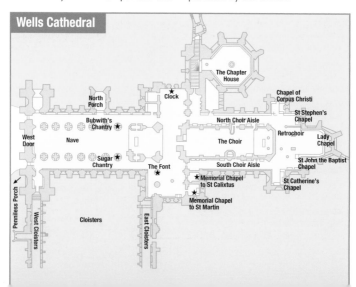

Wells Cathedral

- The Chapter House
- Clock
- Chapel of Corpus Christi
- St Stephen's Chapel
- North Porch
- Bubwith's Chantry
- North Choir Aisle
- Retrochoir
- Lady Chapel
- West Door
- Nave
- The Choir
- Sugar Chantry
- The Font
- South Choir Aisle
- St John the Baptist Chapel
- Memorial Chapel to St Calixtus
- St Catherine's Chapel
- Penniless Porch
- West Cloisters
- Cloisters
- East Cloisters
- Memorial Chapel to St Martin

Above: carvings of the Apostles at the top of the west facade.

Walk past the memorial chapels to St Calixtus and St Martin and head for the Choir. This is the heart of the cathedral and one of the oldest parts. On the underside of the seats are elaborately carved misericords (to support the clerics during periods in the service when they are required to stand). The east window (1340) depicts the lineage of Christ, with Jesse, King David (son of Jesse) and Mary *(see box below)*. High up above

the Choir are small niches where boy sopranos would have played the part of angels on feast days.

At the South Choir Aisle, there are a number of important tombs: on the left (moving east), the Tomb of Bishop Harewell (1380); the effigies of three Saxon Bishops, whose bones were transferred here from the Saxon cathedral in around 1200, when Wells was trying to regain cathedral status for the church of St Andrew; and

F The Jesse Window

This magnificent east window dates from about 1340. It is considered one of the best examples of 14th-century stained glass in the world. The cathedral escaped destruction in the Reformation, during the Civil War and World War II. Urgent repair and conservation, however, was deemed necessary so the Jesse Window Project was launched and work began in 2011 after £500,000 was raised. Meticulous cleaning and conservation work is still underway, gradually restoring the glass to its original glory.

Above: view up to the Jesse Window.

the good Bishop Bekynton's tomb, with its grim reminder of death (the bishop's corpse rotting in his shroud) on the bottom rung. Bekynton, Bishop of Bath and Wells from 1443–65, built the choir school over the West Cloister, the Chain Bridge and, for the people of Wells, a row of 12 houses in the marketplace. At the eastern end of the aisle are three examples of carved misericords.

Stained glass

Next is St Catherine's Chapel, where the stained glass was salvaged from a church in Rouen (desecrated during the French Revolution) in 1813, and St John the Baptist Chapel. The Lady Chapel, built in 1326, was originally a separate building. The Lady Chapel windows were shattered during the Civil War (1642–47) and Monmouth's Protestant Rebellion (1685). Only the upper sections contain the original glass. The brass lectern at the entrance to the Lady Chapel was given by Dean Robert Creyghton to mark the restoration of King Charles II in 1660.

The Retrochoir was built to unite the Lady Chapel with the presbytery. The ribs in the lovely vaulting were decorated by T.H. Willement in 1845. Notice the magnificent 13th-century cope (cloak) chest nearby.

Pass St Stephen's Chapel and the Chapel of Corpus Christi, which is reserved for private prayer, and make for the North Choir Aisle. Among the tombs are that of Bishop Giso (d.1088), brought here from the Saxon cathedral, and the alabaster tomb of Bishop Ralph of Shrewsbury (d.1363), who founded the College of Vicars and built the Vicars' Hall (see p.95).

The curving flight of steps leading up to the octagonal Chapter House was built in the 13th century. Worn by age and use, the lovely honey-coloured stone is illuminated by windows containing the oldest stained glass in the cathedral. The Chapter House itself, where cathedral business was carried out (and still is today on important occasions), was completed in 1306. Seating for 49 canons lines the walls, each space marked by the name of the estate; above, 32 tierceron ribs (precursor of fan vaulting) spray from a central pier. As you leave the Chap-

Below: Wells Cathedral sits amid delightful grounds.

ter House, a narrow flight of stairs (added in 1459) leads off to the Chain Bridge, which links the cathedral with the Vicar's Hall.

Medieval clock

The medieval clock is one of the treasures of the cathedral. It actually has two faces: one on the exterior wall of the cathedral, the other here. Still keeping time today (though the original internal mechanism is in the Science Museum in London), it is comprised of three dials, the outer one indicating the hours on a 24-hour clockface, the middle one showing the minutes, and the inner one marking the date of the lunar month. Try to catch the clock striking the hour, when jousting knights rotate. This is also the best place to view the beautiful scissor arches, added by master mason William Joy from 1338–48. Though built to solve technical problems – the weight of the tower, enlarged by Dean John Godelee in 1313, was straining the foundations – the visual effect is stunning.

The Cloisters are approached from the south-west side of the nave. Replacing the smaller 13th-century cloisters, they were completed in 1508.

Above: National Trust gift shop, Wells.

Above the East Cloister is the medieval library, financed by a legacy of Bishop Bubwith (d.1424), containing around 6,000 books. A door in the south cloister leads to the Bishop's Palace (also accessible from the marketplace). The cathedral shop is siutated in the Entry Cloister, and the restaurant is in the former choirmaster's house on the first floor.

There's an interpretation centre where you can learn about the area's geographical landscape, the building's history, and the cathedral's ministry. It also reveals behind-the-scenes life at the modern-day cathedral through a series of displays.

Scenes from the Hollywood film *The Other Boleyn Girl* (2008), with Eric Bana as Henry VIII, were filmed in the cathedral, as was *Elizabeth: The Golden Age* (2007), with Cate Blanchett playing Queen Bess.

F King Arthur

In some Arthurian literature, Glastonbury is identified with the legendary island of Avalon, where Arthur's sword Excalibur was forged. An early Welsh poem links Arthur to Glastonbury Tor in an account of a confrontation between Arthur and Melwas, who had kidnapped Queen Guinevere. According to some versions of the Arthurian legend, Lancelot retreated to Glastonbury Abbey in penance following the death of Arthur.

THE BISHOP'S PALACE
The Bishop's Palace (tel: 01749 988111, ext 200; www.bishopspalace wells.co.uk; daily Apr–Oct 10am–6pm, Nov–Dec, Feb–Mar 10am–4pm, occasionally closed for private events;

Above: part of the Bishop's Palace in the cathedral city of Wells.

charge) has been home to the bishops of Bath and Wells for more than 800 years. Work was begun in the early 13th century by Bishop Jocelin and enlarged by successive bishops until the mid-15th century. Moated and approached over a drawbridge, it was clearly designed for defence. Such features were added by Bishop Ralph of Shrewsbury in the 14th century.

The Henderson Rooms form the oldest part of the palace. In the First Floor Hall style, they comprise a ground-floor cellar from which a Jacobean staircase installed by Bishop Montague (1608–16) leads to a suite of state rooms: the Long Gallery, lined with portraits of past bishops, many of whom played key roles in English history; a Victorian-style Drawing Room, overlooking Bishop Jocelin's deer park (now pasture); the Conference Room, with its elaborate plaster ceiling and carpet from Windsor Castle; and Panelled Room, in which portraits of more recent bishops are displayed. Also open to visitors is the adjoining Bishop's Chapel, the private chapel

of the Bishop of Bath and Wells. A Visitor Centre was added in 2012.

As you make your way back to the gatehouse, note the ruins of the Great Hall, built by Bishop Robert Burnell (1275–93). During the Reformation, the hall was the scene of the trial of the abbot and treasurer of Glastonbury Abbey, accused of sedition for their opposition to Henry VIII's severance from the Church of Rome. Found guilty, they were executed on Glastonbury Tor.

For whom the bell tolls

A particular delight for children are the mute swans in the palace moat, which, for the past 150 years, have been ringing a bell at the gatehouse to summon food.

From the gatehouse, a pleasant walk off to the left skirts the grounds of the palace, returning along St Andrew Street on the north side of the cathedral and passing **Vicar's Close**. This charming cobbled close was built in 1348 by Bishop Ralph of Shrewsbury to house 'Members of the College of Vicars', clerics chosen for

F Glastonbury Festival

Glastonbury is the granddaddy of all music festivals. Inspired by the hippie movement, it was started in the early 1970s by farmer Michael Eavis on his fields at Worthy Farm, near Pilton. Glastonbury, or Glasto as it's commonly known, is now the largest green-field open-air music and performing arts festival in the world. As well as hosting some of the biggest names in music, it also features dance, comedy, theatre, circus, cabaret and many other arts.

Above: the Pyramid stage, a permanent structure, hosts the headline acts.

their singing voices. Wander down past the identical cottages with their distinct chimneys and you can easily imagine yourself in some period drama. The houses have been continuously occupied and altered over the years except for No. 22, which has retained its appearance. Over the gate is Vicar's Hall, where members dined, and at the far end of the street is the chapel. Vicar's Hall is joined to

Below: Market Square, Glastonbury.

the cathedral by the Chain Bridge.

Walking past the north side of the cathedral into Cathedral Green be sure to notice the exterior side of the clock, on which two medieval warriors mark time.

Wells and Mendip Museum

Back in the marketplace, on the square's north side is a set of houses built in the 1450s, which are still known as the Nova Opera (New Works). A plaque marks the world-record long jump by Wells resident Mary Rand in 1964. The Wells and Mendip Museum (tel: 01749 673477; www.wells museum.org.uk; Easter–Oct Mon–Sat 10am–5pm, Nov–Easter 11am–4pm; charge) has displays of local history and archaeology, including a new permanent caving exhibition, The Netherworld of Mendip.

GLASTONBURY AND STREET

From Wells, the A39 leads on to **Glastonbury ❷** (population 8,600), the scene for the past 40-plus years of a celebrated annual rock festival in fields nearby, attracting huge crowds to see the biggest names in pop. By contrast, it is also home to the oldest

Above: Glastonbury Tor can be seen for miles around.

Christian foundation in Britain. The ruined **abbey** (www.glastonburyabbey.com; Mar–Oct 9am–6pm, June–Aug until 8pm, Nov–Feb 9am–4pm; charge) is built on the site of a much earlier church which, according to legend, dates from the 1st century, when Joseph of Arimathea is supposed to have brought either the Holy Grail or the Blood of the Cross here. St Patrick and St Bridget visited the abbey in the 5th century, and Edmund I (d.946), Edgar (d.975) and Edmund Ironside (d.1016) are all buried here. The buildings that you see date from between 1184 and 1303, when Glastonbury was the richest Benedictine abbey bar Westminster in England: they fell into ruins after Henry VIII dissolved the monasteries. Remains of a warrior and his female companion, interred in front of the high altar, are identified as King Arthur and Queen Guinevere by local legend. Winter-flowering hawthorns in the abbey's grounds are supposed to have sprung from the Holy Thorn borne here by Joseph. **Glastonbury Tor**, above the town, offers views as far as the Bristol Channel. Despite being an area of myth and legend, the town of Glastonbury itself is rather a disappointment, swamped with shops dabbling in mysticism and New Age healing.

Just south of Glastonbury is **Street**, site of Millfield public school and the headquarters of the shoe company Clark's, founded in 1825 by wool dealer and rug-maker Cyrus Clark, who was soon running a profitable business making wool-lined slippers. Clark's Village (a factory-price outlet for well-known brands) includes a shoe museum.

A return to Bath along the picturesque A361 heads to the historic

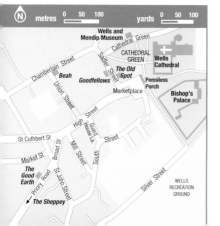

town of **Shepton Mallet** ❸ (9 miles/5km from Glastonbury). Three miles (5km) east of Shepton Mallet at Cranmore is the departure point for the East Somerset Steam Railway (tel: 01749 880417; www.eastsomerset railway.com). From Shepton Mallet, the A37 passes Downside abbey and school to pick up the A367 to Bath via **Radstock** ❹, where Radstock Museum (tel: 01761 437722; www.radstock museum.co.uk; Tue–Fri, Sun and Bank Holiday Mon 2–5pm, Sat 11am–5pm, closed Dec and Jan; charge) recalls 19th-century life in a north Somerset coalfield. The last coal was mined here in 1973.

Above: East Somerset Steam Railway.

ⓔ Eating Out

Beah
2 Union Street; tel: 01749 678111; www.beah.co.uk; Mon–Sat breakfast (from 10am), lunch and dinner. Popular restaurant offering a mix of Moroccan, English and Mediterranean food, such as lamb or chicken tagine, and roasted supreme of pheasant on a bed of chestnut, parsley mash. ££

The Good Earth
4 Priory Road; tel: 01749 678600; www.thegoodearthwells.co.uk; Mon–Fri 9am–4.30pm, Sat 9am–5pm. Just off the High Street is this well-liked vegetarian and vegan restaurant offering simple, cheap and filling fare. It's welcoming and child-friendly with a very homey atmosphere in a rabbit warren of a building. Small courtyard for summer eating. £

Goodfellows
5 Sadler Street; tel: 01749 673866; www.goodfellowswells.co.uk; Wed–Sat lunch and dinner, Tue lunch only. This award-winning restaurant serves fish caught off the Devon and Cornish coasts. Next door is the Sadler Street Café (£–££), a European-style café during the day that serves meat and game-dominated dishes in the evening to contrast with its fish-focused partner. £££

The Old Spot
12 Sadler Street; tel: 01749 689099; www.theoldspot.co.uk; Wed–Sat lunch and dinner, Tue dinner only. Classic French and Italian regional dishes with an emphasis on ingredients you might not see too often, such as offal. Husband-and-wife team Clare and Ian Bates encourage diners to sample items they might not have tried before, such as wild garlic soup, hangar steak with lentils and snails, or hake with samphire. ££–£££

The Sheppey
Lower Godney, Glastonbury; tel: 01458 831594; www.thesheppey.co.uk; daily lunch and dinner. Located between Wells and Glastonbury, this delightful pub overlooks the Somerset Levels. Choose from fish stew to steaks from the Spanish charcoal oven. Snacks and children's menu available, too. ££

The Wookey Hole Inn
High Street, Wookey Hole; tel: 01749 676677; www.wookeyholeinn.com; Mon–Sat lunch and dinner, Sun lunch only. How can you resist a place that offers 'love, peace and great food'? An eccentric laid-back gastro-pub serving inventive, good food. ££

Tour 9

Longleat and Stourhead

This 50-mile (80km) driving tour combines two stately homes – Longleat, known for its splendid safari park, and Stourhead, famed for its landscaped gardens. Allow 1–2 days

The home of the Marquess of Bath, **Longleat** ❶ (22 miles/35km from Bath) is one of the south-west's top tourist attractions. A full day is required for Longleat alone, especially if you want to see the Safari Park too; during school holidays it is advisable to arrive early.

Leave Bath along the A36 and, after about 13 miles (20km), take the A361 heading south to Shepton Mallet. Four miles (7.5km) later, follow the B3092 signed for Longleat.

The house is set in over 900 acres (364 hectares) of parkland, landscaped by Lancelot 'Capability' Brown, with 8,000 acres (3,237 hecatres) of woods and farmland. It was the first stately home to open to the public, and also claims to be

> ## Highlights
> - Longleat House
> - Longleat Safari Park
> - Stourhead
> - St Alfred's Tower

the first safari park outside Africa. There is a range of admission charges at Longleat, depending on which attractions you want to visit. Alongside the house and safari park, there are a number of attractions including an enormous hedge maze, adventure castle, motion simulators, tea-cup ride, King Arthur's Mirror Maze and Postman Pat village. An 'all-in-one' day ticket grants access to all of them. It's also best to ring (tel: 01985 844400) or visit the website (www.longleat.co.uk) to check on opening times (broadly 10am–4pm), as they vary by the seasons. Completely separate from the house and safari park, but occupying 400 acres (162 hectares) of Longleat Forest (off the A36) is Center Parcs (www.centerparcs.co.uk), a family-oriented holiday-village-club-cum-theme-park where the theme is the great outdoors.

THE MARQUESS OF BATH

Henry Thynne, the sixth Marquess of Bath, opened Longleat to the public in 1949, a course of action partly necessitated by heavy death duties imposed after the death of the fifth Marquess in 1946. It was the first stately home to go public, but others soon followed suit. Since then, Longleat has spawned a huge entertainment complex attracting some 850,000 tourists a year. The abiding pleasure of Longleat, however, is the vast parkland. Visitors can roam more or less as they please and fish in the lower reaches of the lake.

Left: Longleat House. *Below*: giraffe being measured at Longleat Safari Park.

The wealthy Thynne family has modest roots. The founder of the dynasty, John Thynne (1515–80), began his working life as a clerk in the kitchen of the Tudor court. His prospects improved dramatically when, under the patronage of the Protector of Somerset, he was made a knight of the realm for his services in a battle against the Scots in 1547. With knighthood came prestige and wealth, and between 1559 and 1580 he built Longleat. His grandson, Thomas Thynne, introduced royal blood to the line through his second marriage to Catherine Lyte Howard, descendant of the First Duke of Norfolk, whose ancestors included Edward I and Alfred the Great. In 1682, Thomas's grandson was made the first Viscount Weymouth, and in 1789 the third Viscount Weymouth was made first Marquess of Bath by George III.

LONGLEAT HOUSE

The house is widely regarded as one of the finest examples of Elizabethan architecture in Britain. The first room you come to on entering the house and turning right from the reception is the Great Hall, a vast panelled room 35ft (11m) high, complete with a min-

Left: Longleat maze, one of the longest hedge mazes in the world.

ry Flemish tapestries), the Italian-style Ante Library and Red Library, containing some of Longleat's 40,000 books, the Breakfast Room, Lower Dining Room (with a Crace ceiling adapted from the Doge's Palace in Venice) and the sumptuous state rooms (dining room, saloon, drawing room and suite of state bedrooms). It was from the State Drawing Room that Titian's *Rest on the Flight to Egypt* was stolen in 1995. The painting was recovered in May 2003 and, after a programme of restoration, has gone back on display.

The unconventional current Marquess passed the management of the business to his son, Viscount Weymouth, in 2010. Morning tours, lasting 40 minutes, are on offer daily. There are also private 'chattel' tours, featuring a variety of artefacts – furniture, paintings and porcelain – normally unseen by the public. Among the attractions in the outbuildings is the Family Bygones exhibition, featuring a collection of everyday objects from 1850 to 1930, belonging to the Estate. Meet the Ancestors is an audio-visual presentation about the Thynne family and their links to royalty.

strels' gallery, which is the one room predominantly from the Elizabethan era; exhibits here include the blood-stained tunic worn by Charles I on his execution. Leading on from here is a series of ornate rooms, impeccably kept but with a comfortable, lived-in quality in spite of the opulence. Much of what you see was created in the Italian style by the designer J.D. Crace for the fourth Marquess of Bath: the Lower East Corridor (fine 17th-centu-

Ⓚ Avon Valley Country Park

This riverside park, about 5 miles (8km) west of Bath at Pixash Lane, Keynsham, provides a foolproof family day out, especially for younger children. There are farm animals, rare breeds, and a Vietnamese pot-bellied pig. Alternatively the kids can head for the indoor or outdoor play areas (with lots of climbing and a scary drop-slide), the quad bikes, miniature railway, boating and fishing, trampolines and pedal go-karts.

Above: an Eagle Owl at the park.

Above: the meerkats of Longleat.

Longleat Safari Park

If you've made the kids trawl through the house, you'll have to make up for it by whisking them around the Safari Park (charge). The park, which opened in 1966 as the first such drive-through park outside Africa, is a 15-minute drive from the house. There is a series of parkland enclosures in which, except in the areas where the animals are fairly harmless (giraffes, zebra, antelopes, etc), you are required to stay in your car with the windows closed (or take one of the special buses).

As you head off on your drive, your first stop allows you to get out of the car at the new African Village where you have the opportunity to see giraffes being fed (10.30–11.30am); watch the antics of zebra, tapirs, wallabies and warthogs; see the spectacular Lemur Walkthrough, accessed via an overhead bridge; climb the majestic baobob tree, and stop for refreshments. Passing by the flamingoes and the vultures, you go on to the Monkey Drive Thru, which can be bypassed

if you are adverse to them leaping all over your car. The Big Game Park has southern white rhinos, Ankole cattle (an ancient breed), camels and ostrich, followed by a deer park. Get a sighting of the recovering elephant, Anne, saved from circus hell, and now free in her own paddock. Then you're into Tiger Territory, showcasing one of the most popular and beautiful animals at the park.

The lions of Longleat

The Bengal tigers are followed by the stars of the show, the Lions of Longleat. It's a genuine thrill to get a close-up look, from the safety of your vehicle, at these powerful and magnificent beasts, which are separated into two prides as lions are naturally territorial. Eight cubs were born in 2012. Also new is Cheetah Kingdom, where you may get a flash of the sleek cats that speed at 70 miles (113km) per hour. On the way out of the park, you'll be able to catch a glimpse of a pack of Canadian timber wolves. Many of the animal species at Longleat are regarded as endangered or rare in the wild.

Back in the Adventure Park there are many more new animal attractions and some old favourites. Go along to Animal Adventure shows for hands-on experiences from tarantulas to guinea pigs; hand-feed the deer, and enter the bat cave if you dare. Check out the Jungle Kingdom, with its Monkey Temple, meerkat walkthrough, anteaters and porcupines. There's the perfect habitat for four lowland gorillas at their lakeside retreat, which you can observe on a jungle cruise. A jungle train ride will pass sea lions and pelicans, and you may possibly glimpse one old silverback gorilla, Nico, on his own island in the lake. And don't miss Penguin Island, where you watch penguins swim beneath your feet in a subterranean cave.

Above: Stourhead's Palladian bridge was based on one in Vicenza, Italy, while the Pantheon beyond it is filled with statues of classical deities.

F Painterly Inspiration

The gardens at Stourhead were designed by Henry Hoare II and laid out between 1741 and 1780 in a classical 18th-century design set around a large lake, achieved by damming a small stream. The inspiration behind their creation was the painters Claude Lorrain, Poussin, and, in particular, Gaspar Dughet, who painted Utopian-type views of landscapes. It is similar in style to the landscape gardens at Stowe House in Buckinghamshire.

Above: Stourhead has one of the finest Regency rooms in England.

STOURHEAD

Head back to the B3092, and follow the signs to **Stourhead** ❷ (house: Apr–Oct daily 11am–4.30pm, Jan–Mar, Nov–Dec Sat–Sun 11am–3pm; garden: daily 9am–7pm or sunset; charge), a Palladian mansion, now owned by the National Trust, built in 1721–24 by Colen Campbell. It's worth spending half a day here.

The estate is famous for its grounds, which represent one of the finest expressions of the early 18th-century landscape movement. A satisfying arrangement of formal gardens, dells, knolls, lake and parkland enfolds temples to Flora and Apollo (seen in the 2005 film version of *Pride and Prejudice*), bridges, a cascade, a Gothic cottage, a grotto and the parish church, creating a delightful theatre for the changing seasons. Horace Walpole thought the gardens here 'one of the most picturesque scenes in the world'.

The grounds are very family-friendly and there's a large programme of family events during the summer. The lake is full of swans and ducks, and the atmospheric grottoes provide plenty of

scope for fun and games. The gardens were shown off in Stanley Kubrick's film *Barry Lyndon*, and a miniature replica of Stourhead House featured as Lady Penelope's residence in the television puppet series *Thunderbirds*.

On the west side of the garden a footpath leads for 2½ miles (4km) to **Alfred's Tower** (Mar–Oct Fri–Tue noon–4pm), an 18th-century brick folly. You can climb the 205 steps to get lovely views over the counties of Wiltshire, Somerset and Dorset, which all meet at this point. You can picnic in the grounds or plan your visit around a trip to the Spread Eagle Inn *(see below)*. Retrace your steps to return to Bath.

E Eating Out

The Angel Inn
Upton Scudamore; tel: 01985 213225; www.theangelinn.co.uk; daily noon–2pm and 6–9pm.
This country inn, about 5 miles (8km) from Longleat on the edge of Salisbury Plain, has a relaxed, informal feel with a walled garden and a terrace offering alfresco dining in summer. The cooking is inventive, featuring seared fillets of sea bass on organic buckwheat noodles with tiger prawn wantons. ££

The Bath Arms
Clay Street, Crockerton; tel: 01985 212262; www.batharmscrockerton. co.uk; daily noon–2pm and 6.30–9pm.
Despite its traditional look, the food in this 17th-century coaching inn close to Longleat has a modern approach with warm duck salad with beetroot and capers and fillet of black bream with smoked haddock chowder. Good bar snacks, too. ££

The George at Nunney
Church Street, Nunney; tel: 01373 836458; www.thegeorgeatnunney. co.uk; Mon–Sat noon–2–5pm, 6.30–9pm, Sun noon–3pm.
In a pretty village near Frome, the George has been refurbished to a high standard. The quality food is British modern, with Asian and Mediterranean influences. Specials such as a pizza with a glass of wine are offered. ££

Spread Eagle
Stourhead Estate; tel: 01747 840587; www.spreadeagleinn.com; food daily 8–9am, noon–3pm and 7–9pm.
This delightful 18th-century pub has excellent locally sourced food, real ales brewed in a nearby village and cosy log fires in winter. Try the popular Wiltshire ploughman's lunch, or splash out in the evening on West Country rump steak. There's also a licensed National Trust restaurant with freshly prepared dishes incorporating food from Stourhead's own walled garden, tenant farmers and local suppliers. ££

Walnut Tree Inn
Shaftsbury Road, Mere; tel: 01747 861220; www.walnut-tree-inn.co.uk; food served daily noon–9pm.
Just 3 miles (5km) southeast of Stourhead, this flower-bedecked, friendly pub with rooms serves reasonably priced, well-sourced pub food. Also Sunday carvery and breakfast Mon–Sat 8–11.30am. £–££

Tour 10

The Ancient Sites (Stonehenge and Avebury)

An 85-mile (135km) round trip taking in the ancient sites of Stonehenge and Avebury. The driving should take about 2½ hours and you will need a whole day for the excursion

The full tour takes in Stonehenge, one of the most iconic and mysterious sights in the world, the magical stone circle at Avebury and other ancient sites, including Silbury Hill. If you are pushed for time, you can simply do a round trip from Bath to Stonehenge (45 miles/72km).

STONEHENGE

From **Bath ❶**, the A36 leads south to Warminster (population: 17,000) and then, 17 miles (27km) further on, to Salisbury Plain, on which looms Britain's most evocative ancient monument, **Stonehenge ❷** (daily June–Aug 9am–7pm, mid-Mar–May and Sept–mid-Oct 9.30am–6pm, mid-Oct–mid-Mar

9.30am–4pm; charge, free to English Heritage and National Trust members), a Unesco World Heritage Site, which attracts around 900,000 visitors a year. The stone circle at Stonehenge is one of the most iconic sights in the world and has featured in numerous films and TV series, from *Doctor Who* (2010) to *Tess of the D'Urbervilles* (1979 and 2008), and *The Black Knight* (1954)

ⓕ Coach Tours

If you don't have a car, several companies offer tours of Stonehenge, Avebury and other sights. **Mad Max Tours** (www.madmax.abel. co.uk) takes you to Stonehenge and Avebury, Silbury Hill, the White Horse and the beautiful villages of Lacock (see p.70) and Castle Combe (see p.73). **Scarper Tours** (www. scarpertours.com) offers what it calls the Ultimate Stonehenge Tour, a three-hour scenic round trip with at least one hour at Stonehenge, and views of chalk hill carvings, ancient burial mounds, Celtic hill forts and thatched villages. Both tours depart daily from Orange Grove in Bath.

Left and Above: Stonehenge and summer solstice celebrations.

to *Stonehenge Apocalypse* (2010) and *Thor: The Dark World* (2013).

Follow the A36, then head east on the A303 towards Amesbury and follow signs to Stonehenge.

Early history

Stonehenge was built as a temple – at first just a circular ditch and bank, within which lay a circle of upright timber posts. This was constructed about 5,000 years ago in the Neolithic period. By about 2,500BC, more timber structures had been built and rotted away, and the first stones had started to arrive. The huge sarsen stones (extremely hard-wearing sandstone) were found scattered among the downs

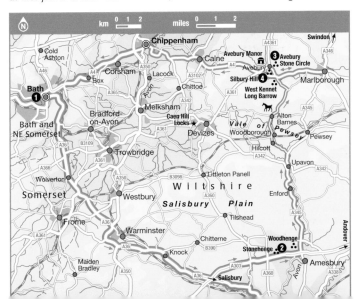

Above: Stonehenge – how the stones were transported here is still a mystery.

of Salisbury Plain in Wiltshire, while the smaller bluestones came from the Preseli Mountains in Pembrokeshire, west Wales, 200 miles (320km) away. This marked the start of eight centuries of construction and alteration stretching into the Bronze Age, when the first metal tools and weapons were made. By this time, Stonehenge was the greatest temple in Britain, its banks, ditches and standing stones arranged in sophisticated alignments to mark the passage of the sun and the changing seasons.

Its purpose has baffled archaeologists and other experts for centuries and engendered many myths. The architect Inigo Jones, one of the first to investigate its purpose, at the behest of King James I, said it could not have been built by the native Britons because they were 'savage and barbarous'. He concluded, instead, that it was a Roman temple to Uranus. Though the alignment of the major axis with the midsummer sunrise suggests a religious purpose, no firm evidence has been found, and theories range from the practical – a calendar – to the magical, usually involving the wizard Merlin, to the extraterrestrial. In March 2013 studies of some 50,000 cremated bones from 63 individuals buried at Stonehenge revealed they long predate the monument in its current form, indicating its significance as a burial site. Work by scientists from several English universities is ongoing and excavations continue.

Protecting the site

In 1883, Stonehenge gained recognition as a monument of national importance. In 1901, the site was fenced off, amid protests, to allow restoration work. In 1915, somewhat remarkably, Stonehenge was bought at auction for £6,600 by local man Cecil Chubb, who subsequently presented it to the government. From 1919, more restoration work was undertaken alongside excavations of the whole site. In 1950, further excavations and investigations were launched, with carbon dating giving an accurate picture of the age of Stonehenge for the first time.

Although it was fenced off at the start of the 20th century, visitors were allowed to wander among the stones for many years. By 1978, visitor numbers had risen so dramatically that a decision was taken to restrict access to

the stones, which are roped off, though today's visitors can still get a good view of the imposing monument.

Around the stones

You can take a tour with a free audio-guide (available in 10 languages) to learn more about the history and legends surrounding the inspirational site. You can also explore the prehistoric landscape around the circle.

The most visible elements of Stonehenge are the majestic stones. Some are small, unshaped or broken, but many are massive, finely worked

and intact. The central cluster has a jumbled appearance but its stones were once arranged in a series of circular and horseshoe-shaped patterns. Other isolated stones used to have companions, which have since vanished. It's thought that more than half the stones may have been lost, probably being reused for building work.

Ancient mystery

One of the mysteries of Stonehenge is how the stones got to Salisbury Plain from so far away. Experiments have shown that the bigger sarsen stones can be dragged on a simple wooden sledge running on wooden rails by a team of about 200 people. It's estimated that it would take about 12 days to drag a stone from the Marlborough Downs to Stonehenge. Though the bluestones are smaller, they had much further to travel (200 miles/330km) and their route is still a matter of debate, possibly being transported on water as well as by land.

In their final arrangement, the stones were arranged in four concentric settings, two circles and two of horseshoe shape. Even after 4,000 years of decay, these structures can still be recognised today. The outermost setting was originally a circle of 30 of the large, up-

F Caen Hill Flight of Locks

The impressive flight of 29 locks at Caen Hill, near Devizes, was one of the most remarkable feats of engineering when the Kennet and Avon Canal was built. The 29 locks over 2 miles (3.2km) was engineer John Rennie's solution to climbing a very steep hill, and was the last part of the canal's 87-mile (145km) route to be completed. Queen Elizabeth II visited the locks when the canal was officially reopened in 1990.

Above: it takes about 5 hours to transport a barge through the locks.

Above: Avebury Stone Circle, one of the largest neolithic monuments in Europe.

right sarsen stones, with 17 remaining, topped by horizontal stones, of which five remain in place. The inner section, a horseshoe of five huge sarsen structures, is the most impressive with each structure resembling a great doorway. One of the sarsens here is the tallest standing stone in Britain at more than 24ft (7m) high.

Magical alignment

At Stonehenge, on the longest day of the year (21 June), the sun rises behind the Heel Stone, one of two sarsens that once stood outside the main entrance to the enclosure, and its rays shine into the heart of the stones. The way Stonehenge is arranged has been seen as evidence that it was designed to mark the summer solstice, the mid-point of summer. People flock every year to Stonehenge to witness this sunrise, though the vagaries of the British weather have been known to spoil the party. The sunset at the winter solstice, the shortest day of the year, occurs on the exact opposite side of the horizon from the midsummer sunrise. One theory is that Stonehenge was built to mark not the

longest day, but the shortest, which marked the return of lighter days after a period of darkness and fear in prehistoric times.

Despite its popularity as a tourist attraction, the facilities at Stonehenge were often a disappointment to many visitors, with an intrusive carpark, crowds battling for a good view and no decent exhibitions. English Heritage's ambitious £27 million project started in 2010 has, however, seen a transfor-

F Myths of Stonehenge

A number of tall tales has arisen around Stonehenge. According to one, the Devil bought the stones from a woman in Ireland, wrapped them up, and brought them to Salisbury plain. Stonehenge is also associated with Arthurian legend. It is said that Merlin the wizard directed the henge's removal from Ireland, where it had been constructed on Mount Killaraus by Giants. King Arthur's father, Uther Pendragon, is supposedly buried inside the ring of stones.

Above: painting the sacred stones.

mation not only in facilities and exhibitions but in the entire landscape of the area. The new low-level, environmentally friendly visitor centre, located 1½ miles (2km) from the stones, features high-quality exhibitions and education facilities, plus a café and large shop. A low-key visitor transit system to the stones keeps cars away from the site, thus enhancing the magical ambience of the area, making for a much less intrusive visit.

The closure of the A344, which passed close to the stones, will further protect the World Heritage Site, with the whole area being grassed over. The Neolithic Houses Project will see three houses built at the centre, using archaeological evidence and authentic materials to see how people lived 4,500 years ago. The project will be undertaken in 2014 and volunteers will assist in the building.

Access to the stone circle is normally restricted, but it is possible to request a special tour, allowing you to walk among the stones (tel: 01722 343834; www.english-heritage.org. uk/stonehenge). This must be done by advance booking.

AVEBURY

If Stonehenge has whetted your appetite for Britain's ancient history but you want to be able to get really close to some ancient stones and to touch them, head to **Avebury Stone Circle ❸** (free admission to view stones, dawn–dusk), the largest circle in Britain.

From the A303 at Stonehenge, take a left onto the A345 towards Marlborough. On the left you will see signs for the significant Bronze Age site of Woodhenge, a henge and timber circle without the pulling power of its more famous neighbour. From the A345 heading north, head off the A roads and follow signs for Hilcott and Woodborough, where you will be able to see one of Wiltshire's famous white horses carved on to the chalk hillside on the right. Carry on to West Overton until you reach the A4, when you should head west towards Calne and follow signs to Avebury.

The magic of Avebury

The stones at Avebury were hauled from the Marlborough Downs, 3 miles (5km) away, some 4,500 years ago. The sarsen stones form one large circle surrounded by a ditch (originally twice as deep as it is today) and two sets of smaller concentric circles (spanned by Avebury village which has grown up among the stones so you will find the Red Lion pub in the middle, see p.111, along with a shop). It is believed the large circle originally had between 95 and 108 stones, some weighing in excess of 40 tons each. The site was used for ceremonialpurposes, a role revived by Druids and New Agers at the winter and summer solstices and spring and autumn equinoxes. A concrete post in the centre of an inner circle marks the spot of the obelisk, a tall thin stone around which human bones have been found. After 10 centuries

Ⓕ Silbury Hill

It is believed that Silbury was built in four stages with only human muscle, antler horns and other basic tools such as oxen shoulder blades used to pile up its million cubic yards of chalk. The completed mound, at 130ft (39m), is one of the largest man-made hills in Europe. The reason for its construction remains a mystery despite a series of excavations beginning in the 18th century.

of service, the site fell into disuse and eventually became a quarry. Many of the original stones were used for building work, including some of the structures in Avebury itself.

In some ways, Avebury could not be more different than Stonehenge. While Stonehenge is far more visually impressive, the understandable desire to protect the monument means that visitors can feel distanced from it. At Avebury, you can walk among the stones and touch them. You can sit down in the fields and gaze down at the stones while having a picnic, watching as other visitors kick a football around or play frisbee among the stones. As you walk around the perimeter, you get a sense of the scale of the stone circle and it's possible to find a quiet spot where you can contemplate the majesty and the mystery of the stones in peace.

Avebury Manor

The delightful village of Avebury is also home to the Alexander Keiller Museum, the Barn Gallery and **Avebury Manor** (charge; free to National Trust members). The house is a late 16th-century building with Queen Anne alterations and the house has had many owners. In 2012, the manor underwent a major transformation and featured in the BBC programme *The Manor Reborn*, fronted by Penelope Keith and Paul Martin. Detailed research was undertaken into the lives of the owners and into period interiors, restoring the rooms to reflect the manor's inhabitants. The overgrown Victorian kitchen garden was transformed and features unusual heritage vegetables, as well as modern varieties, which are used in the Circle Café. The museum displays some of the spectacular prehistoric artefacts discovered by Alexander Keiller, the marmalade heir, who spent his family fortune on his passion for archaeology, spending the 1920s

Below: grass now covers the ancient chalk mound of Silbury Hill.

Right: the West Kennet Long Barrow Tomb is estimated 5,000 years old.

and 1930s excavating the Avebury area. The Barn Gallery is a dedicated children's space, with interactive models and computers where children can discover more about Avebury and the Stone Age.

SILBURY HILL

As you return to the A4 from Avebury, a small distance east towards Marlborough the road passes the mysterious **Silbury Hill** ❹ *(see box, opposite)* and, signposted across fields, West Kennet Long Barrow Tomb, *c*.5,000 years old and one of the largest chambered tombs in Britain. Access is allowed into part of the tomb, where votive offerings to Pan are sometimes found – an ear of wheat, a daisy, a lighted candle.

You can carry on a few miles to the attractive market town of Marlborough, whose colonnaded high street offers a lively central market and a clutch of good tea shops popular with pupils at the town's famous public school. To return to Bath, follow the A4 west to Calne, Chippenham and then Bath.

Ⓔ Eating Out

The Harrow at Little Bedwyn
Little Bedwyn; tel: 01672 870871; www.theharrowatlittlebedwyn.com; Wed–Sat lunch and dinner.
Close to Marlborough and Avebury, the Harrow has held a Michelin star for several years in a row, in recognition of its excellent, locally sourced food featuring an original teaming of flavours and textures. Menus to choose from include 7-course gourmet, 4-course tasting, à la carte, and set dinner and lunch, all with specially selected matched wines. £££

Red Lion
High Street, Avebury; tel: 01672 539266; www.red-lion-pub-avebury. co.uk; food daily 11am–10pm.
This 400-year-old thatched cottage lies within Avebury's ancient stone circle. The reasonable pub grub features mixed grill, beef and ale pie, fish and chips and grilled gammon steak. Children's menu available. ££

Ship Inn
High Street, Upavon; tel: 01980 630130; daily lunch and dinner.
Charming thatched village pub on the A345 on the way to Avebury. Good value pub 'favourites' include fish and chips and sausage and mash, but with some more sophisticated dishes on the menu, too. Handmade pizzas from the wood-fired oven on Thur–Sat evenings. Sticky toffee pudding to die for. ££

Silks on the Downs
Main Road, Ogbourne St Andrew, near Marlborough; tel: 01672 841229; www.silksonthedowns.co.uk; Mon–Sat lunch and dinner, Sun lunch only.
The unusual name comes from this award-winning gastro-pub's links with Wiltshire's rich horse-racing heritage. There are framed silks adorning some of the walls inside. Dishes include wild mushroom risotto, Thai fishcakes and rump of lamb. ££

Travel Tips

Active Pursuits

There's no excuse not to get active in Bath, which is a great city to walk around and has plenty of hills to tackle along the way. There are plenty of other activities to try while you're there, including the chance to soar into the skies in a hot-air balloon, paddling a canoe out on the river, heading for the golf courses in and around the city or just taking in a game of Bath's favourite sport, rugby.

WALKING

Bath's proximity to beautiful countryside makes it easy to head off on walks without needing to get in a car first. Try the Bath Skyline walk (route available from the National Trust website, www.nationaltrust.org.uk), the Bath to Bristol railway path, or follow the River Avon Trail, starting at Pulteney Weir and taking in wooded valleys, water meadows and other places of interest (www.riveravon trail.org.uk). Opened in April 2013, the Two Tunnels Greenway (www. twotunnels.org.uk), a 4-mile (6km) disused railway line has provided an exciting new walking and cycle route, linking Bath with Midford.

BALLOONING

One of the most memorable ways to see Bath is from a hot-air balloon. The family-run Bath Balloons (tel: 01225 466888; www.bathballoons. co.uk) operates year-round. Balloons are launched from Royal Victoria Park and you can help prepare the balloon for take-off *(see box, p.35)*. Flights last about 1 hour (where you end up depends on the wind direction) and include a complimentary glass of champagne. Flights are also available with the Ascent Balloon Company (tel: 01761 432327; www.ascent-balloon. co.uk), Balloons Over Bath (tel: 0845 337 1566; www.go-ballooning.co.uk)

or Devon and Somerset Balloons (tel: 0845 4564 201; www.devonand somersetballoons.co.uk).

BOATING

On the Avon, the Boating Station (Forester Road, tel: 01225 312900; www.bathboating.co.uk) hires out traditional wooden rowing boats, punts and canoes by the hour or day (Easter–Sept daily 10am–6pm). Organised river trips run to Bathampton Weir and back (1 hour) from below Pulteney Bridge.

The Bath and Dundas Canal Co (Brass Knocker Bottom, Monkton Combe; tel: 01225 722292; www. bathcanal.com), 5 miles (8km) southeast of Bath (off the A36), is a historic boatyard where you can hire self-drive electric boats and Canadian canoes for a day or half-day. Bike hire is also available.

Bath Narrowboat Trips (tel: 01225 447276; www.bath-narrowboats.co. uk) provides boats you can hire for the day to navigate your way along the Kennet and Avon canal.

CAVING AND CLIMBING

Cheddar Gorge and Caves (tel: 01934 742343; www.cheddargorge. co.uk) runs caving and climbing expeditions for anyone 11 years and over.

Preceding Pages: relaxing in Parade Gardens. Left: balloons over Bath. Above: cycling along the towpath.

Full equipment is provided. Climbing sessions are available at Bristol Climbing Centre (tel: 0117 9083491; www. undercover-rock.com), an indoor venue with some of the best facilities in the country.

CYCLING

There are plenty of great cycle routes in and around the city. Bath and North East Somerset Council produces maps and guides to help cyclists to plan their journeys and find the best routes. The maps are available free of charge from local libraries and most council offices. You can also get maps and suggested routes from www.betterbybike.info. Further routes and maps are available from Sustrans (www.sustrans.org.uk).

FISHING

Chew and Blagdon lakes, off the A368 west of Bath, offer good fly-fishing for rainbow and brown trout from Mar–Oct. Boats may be hired for the day (book in advance). Though the lakes are popular with experienced anglers, novices are welcome, with beginners' days, casting lessons and tuition weeks available (tel: 01275 332339; www. bristolwater.co.uk/leisure/chew wood-info.asp).

GOLF

Bath Golf Club (tel: 01225 463834; www.bathgolfclub.org.uk) at Sham Castle, Bath's famous folly built by Ralph Allen, is an 18-hole course open to non-members (with handicap certificate) during the week and at weekends (subject to availability); equipment may be hired. Check the dress code.

Bowood House (tel: 01249 823881; www.bowood-golf.co.uk) outside Bath also offers an 18-hole golf course, set in Capability Brown's Bowood Great Park. Open to non-members.

If you're not an expert and you just fancy a hack with the kids, head for the nine-hole golf course at Entry Hill (tel: 01225 834248; www.aquaterra. org/entry-hill-golf-course) in Bath. Everyone is welcome to play but booking is advisable. The Bath Approach Golf Course on Weston Road (tel: 01225 331162; www.aquaterra. org/bath-approach-golf-course) has 30 par-3 holes of varying length and is good for beginners.

ICE-SKATING

The Bristol Ice Rink (tel: 0117 929 2148; www.jnlbristol.co.uk) is open daily for experienced and novice skaters alike. Family sessions on Sunday mornings. Learn to dance on ice.

PONY TREKKING

Wellow Trekking Centre (tel: 01225 834376; www.wellowtrekking.com) is at Little Horse Croft Farm in Wellow, 6 miles (10km) outside Bath. A range of rides is available for adults and children. Open year-round, except Christmas Day.

RIVER CRUISES

Pulteney Weir is one the starting points for river cruises along the Avon. The *Pulteney Princess*, run by Avon Cruising (tel: 07791 910650; www.pulteney princess.co.uk), operates from April

ⓕ Bath Half Marathon

If you turn up in Bath on a Sunday morning in early March, don't be too surprised to find the city's streets closed to traffic and replaced with streams of runners of varying degrees of fitness. The Bath Half Marathon, or the Bath Half as it's commonly known, was launched in 1981 and is one of the longest established and most popular city centre road events in the UK. It raises about £1.5m a year for charity.

to October, offering a 60-minute trip from the bridge upriver to the pretty village of Bathampton. Bath City Boat Trips (tel: 07974 560197; www.bath cityboattrips.com) run 40-minute daily tours with frequent departures (weather permitting) and also special tours of one to four hours with commentary by a Blue Badge Guide. The Bath Small Green Boat Company (tel: 01225 460831) operates an electric boat for green trips along the river in the summer. There are also dining cruises on *The Penny Lane*, moored next to the leisure centre.

OUTDOOR SWIMMING

If you want an outdoor pool, head for Bristol Lido (tel: 0117 933 9530; www.lidobristol.com), built in 1849 and renovated ahead of its reopening in 2008. Ideal on a summer's day, though the entry rules are difficult to grasp and it's expensive. On busy days, the Lido limits entry to non-members, so check in advance. For a more affordable dip, head to Portishead Open Air Pool (tel: 01275 843454; www. portisheadopenairpool.org.uk) in this Bristol suburb. The 108ft (33m) main pool in this 1960s modernist building is heated and there are views over the Severn estuary.

Themed Holidays

As such a beautiful city with a long history of the finer things in life such as food and art, Bath is an ideal venue for trying to pick up a new skill with a themed break.

COOKERY

Bath is home to Demuths, one of the country's finest vegetarian restaurants. Its owner Rachel Demuth runs a Vegetarian Cookery School (tel: 01225 427938; www.vegetarian cookeryschool.com) at Terrace Walk in the centre of Bath with views of the Abbey and a superb kitchen. There's a varied selection of courses, for beginners or accomplished cooks, and a wide range of world foods to get your teeth into, such as Thai and Vietnamese, Indian, Moroccan, Mediterranean, Italian, Spanish and Middle Eastern.

Owned and run by French chef and baker, Richard Bertinet, the Bertinet Kitchen (tel: 01225 445531; www.the bertinetkitchen.com) offers a range of relaxed and fun courses for food-lovers of all abilities. Most popular are Bertinet's breadmaking courses, based on his award-winning book *Dough*. You can even spend five days learning how to make bread the Ber-

tinet way, and also find out how to make ice creams and sauces. There are classes where you can learn about knife skills and carving, pasta making or Indian street food and a pastry masterclass, as well as classes for kids. Bertinet's book has sold over 100,000 copies and has been translated into seven languages.

PHOTOGRAPHY

With its stunning buildings and lovely countryside, Bath is a great place to hone your photographic skills. The Royal Photographic Society (tel: 01225 325733; www.rps.org), based at 122 Wells Road, offers workshops open to non-members. You can learn about studio portraiture, wedding photography, nature photography, Photoshop, and how to use a digital SLR camera. Alternatively, you can try Bath with Spirit photographic courses (www.capturethespirit.co.uk), run by one of the country's leading location photographers. Neill Menneer will guide you around the city, showing you how to take more interesting pictures, and offering technical tips and practical advice. He also runs courses on studio portraits and Photoshop.

SPA

With its rejuvenating springs, Bath is the perfect place to go for a pampering spa break. Bath's modern Thermae Bath Spa (tel: 01225 331234; www.thermae bathspa.com) offers a variety of relaxation packages, including a traditional full body massage to relieve everyday tension. Experience the warming Kraxen stove treatment and an Aromatic Moor Mud Wrap. Many hotels, such as Harington's *(see p.123)*, offer special deals combining a luxury stay with a relaxing session at the spa.

Above: the open-air pool at the luxurious Thermae Spa.

Practical Information

GETTING THERE

By train

First Great Western (www.firstgreat western.co.uk) operates a fast service between London Paddington and Bath Spa (from 1hr 30 mins) and Bristol Temple Meads (1hr 45 mins). These run twice an hour Monday to Saturday (less frequent in the later evening) and every hour on Sunday. Generally, the earlier you book your tickets, the cheaper they will be. South West Trains operates less frequent services to Bath from London Waterloo, which are generally cheaper but take longer (around 2 hrs 15 mins). For all rail enquiries contact National Rail Enquiries (tel: 0845 748 4950; www.nationalrail.co.uk).

Bath Spa Station is to the south of the city centre (an eight-minute walk from the Abbey). It has a taxi rank and is close to the city's bus station.

By air

The nearest airport is Bristol (north of the city, near the junction of the M4 and M5 motorways). The airport (tel: 0871 334 4444; www.bristolairport. co.uk), 20 miles (33km) from Bath, has undergone significant expansion over the past decade and is still growing, serving an ever-wider set of destinations. A regular shuttle bus operates between the airport and Bristol city centre and Bristol Temple Meads railway station, where you can catch trains to Bath (about 1 hr in total). Alternatively, you can take a taxi to Bath (about 45 mins). London's Heathrow Airport (www.heathrowairport. com) is 100 miles (160km) east of Bath near the M4 motorway. National Express Coaches run direct services from the airport to Bath (about 2 hrs, 30 mins), or you can catch the Hea-throw Express to London Paddington and catch the train to Bath. This is a quicker (2 hrs 15 mins) but more expensive option.

By car

Bath lies within easy reach of both the M4 and M5 motorways, making it easily accessible from London, Wales and the Midlands. However, the lovely countryside around the city can make slower 'A' roads more attractive options, in particular the A4 across the Wiltshire Downs and the A46 which winds through the Cotswolds from Stroud and Cheltenham.

By coach

National Express runs a direct coach service between London Victoria bus station and Bath every 1–1½ hours, as well as services from many other towns and cities. The journey from London takes about 3 hours (tel: 0871 781 8178; www.nationalexpress.com) but is cheaper than the train. The

Above: the city's narrow streets are not especially traffic-friendly.

coaches arrive at Bath's bus station on Dorchester Street, close to the railway station and a short walk from the centre.

GETTING AROUND
Public transport
Though unlikely to be necessary in the city centre, buses can be useful for making short trips to sites such as Beckford's Tower, Prior Park, the American Museum at Claverton and nearby villages, or further afield to Bristol and Wells. The main bus company in Bath is First Group (tel: 0845 606 4446; www.firstgroup.com) and there is an information point at the main bus station in Dorchester Street. You can buy a ticket as you enter the bus (having change helps), and returns are cheaper than two singles. There are off-peak fares and special offer tickets available.

The open-top bus tours (www. bathbuscompany.com), which offer an all-day hop on and off service, can be a useful way of getting around and seeing the main attractions. The guided tours (charge), which aim to be entertaining as well as informative, set off from High Street (opposite Parade Gardens). Disabled access.

Going green
Bath and North East Somerset Council (tel: 01225 394041; www.bathnes. gov.uk) runs a park-and-ride scheme, so if you're based just outside the centre, you can leave your car on the outskirts and take a bus into the heart of the city. There are three park-and-ride locations: Lansdown in the north of Bath; Newbridge to the west; and Odd Down in the south. Parking is free and you pay for the bus journey to the city centre.

There are some cycle paths in Bath but not enough to offer consistently safe cycling around the city. The ca-

Above: the hop-on, hop-off buses offer an easy way to see the sights.

nal towpath offers a better alternative where possible and there is an excellent cycle path to Bristol. The council is to spend more money to improve the safety and facilities for cyclists in the city.

If you're a member of the City Car Club's car share scheme (tel: 0845 330 1234; www.citycarclub.co.uk) in another part of the country, you can use your card to book and pick up a vehicle from one of about a dozen different locations in and around the city centre. Many of the vehicles are Toyota Prius hybrids.

Trains
Trains to Bristol Temple Meads (not Bristol Parkway, which is some way from the city centre) leave from Bath Spa Station throughout the day and take about 15–25 minutes depending on the type of train. Contact National Rail Enquiries (tel: 0845 748 4950; www.nationalrail.co.uk). Look out for special passes that offer all-day travel on First Group trains and buses.

Driving
When Bath was growing at an alarming rate in the 18th century, it wasn't designed with the combustion engine in mind. As a result, Bath has an

uneasy relationship with the motor car and driving within the city can be a chore, marked by confusing one-way systems, traffic jams and eye-watering parking charges. If possible, leave the car at home or at your hotel. The city centre is compact and most attractions can easily be reached on foot.

Parking is available all over the city, with a dozen or so car parks, but there is limited on-street parking and it's often restricted (some of it valid only for residents, so read the signs carefully as Bath's traffic wardens are very assiduous). Illegally parked cars will be clamped or removed. The main car parks are at Avon Street, Charlotte Street, Walcot Street, the Podium shopping centre, Broad Street, Manvers Street, the Sports Centre, Sainsbury's (Green Park) and the Southgate centre.

Car rental

It is worth hiring a car if you want to explore the countryside and villages around Bath outlined in the tours. Rental firms include Enterprise (tel: 01225 443311), Europcar (tel: 0871 384 9985), Hertz (tel: 0843 309 3004), Kingsmead Motors (tel: 01225 402234) and National Car Rental (tel: 01225 481898).

Taxis

Taxi ranks are found at Bath Spa Station, Orange Grove (next to the Abbey), Milsom Street and Henry Street. It is wise to book in advance on Friday and Saturday evenings. Firms include Abbey Taxis (tel: 01225 444444), V Cars (tel: 01225 464646), Orange Grove Taxis (tel: 01225 447777) and Widcombe Cars (tel: 01225 422610).

Bike hire

Bath By Cycle (3 George's Place; tel: 01225 807881; www.bathbycycle. com) offer traditional and electric bikes for adults and children. The Bath and Dundas Canal Company (tel: 01225 722292; www.bathcanal. com) has adult and children's bikes, plus tagalongs, buggy trailers and child seats. The towpath of the Kennet and Avon Canal offers easy, safe cycling, and there is the wonderful Bath to Bristol cycle route. The Two Tunnels Greenway enables cyclists to complete an almost level circular 13-mile (21km) route, with a 1-mile (2km) long tunnel ride.

FACTS FOR THE VISITOR

Disabled travellers

Though a Georgian city centre doesn't

Below: navigating the city's historic streets.

lend itself to access for the disabled, the council does operate a blue badge scheme for disabled car drivers. Designated bays are available in most city-centre car parks and on the streets.

Shopmobility (3–4 Manvers Street; tel: 01225 481744; Mon–Thu 8.30am–5pm, Fri–Sat 8.30am–4.30pm) hires out manual or powered wheelchairs and electric scooters for nominal cost; formal ID is needed for first registration. It is possible to hire manual wheelchairs overnight. It also offers an escort service, if you prefer a companion on your trip, which is open to people with a sensory or mobility impairment.

Wheelchair-accessible cabs are available from Abbey Taxis (tel: 01225 444444), Somerset Taxis (tel: 01761 411234) and V Cars (tel: 01225 464646).

Above: Guildhall Market.

Emergencies

Police, ambulance, fire brigade: 999 (for emergencies only).
Bath Police Station, Manvers Street; tel: 101; www.avonandsomersetpolice.uk.
NHS Walk-in Centre, Riverside Health Centre, James Street West; tel: 01225 478811; daily 8am–8pm (no appointment necessary).
Bath's main hospital with a casualty unit is Royal United Hospital, Combe Park; tel: 01225 428331.

Opening hours

Standard business hours are 9am–5.30pm, though some shops won't open until 10am and may close at 6pm. Shops offer late-night shopping on Thursday (normally until 6.30pm, but until 8pm in the run-up to Christmas). On Sundays, most shops are only allowed to open for six hours (usually 11am–5pm). Though most museums and sights in Bath are open year-round, many attractions in the countryside are open only between March and Octo-

ber or have restricted opening times in winter. Before planning a trip, be sure to check the opening times of the sights you want to see.

Tourist information

The Tourist Information Centre is located in Abbey Church Yard. The staff can help with a wide range of enquiries about both Bath and the surrounding area, and offer a room booking service. Information, tel: 0906 711 2000 (50p a minute); accommodation, tel: 0844 847 5256. Opening hours Mon–Sat 9.30am–5.30pm, Sun 10am–4pm.

Left luggage

Neither the railway station nor the bus station offers left luggage facilities. However, Backpackers, a friendly hostel at 13 Pierrepont Street (tel: 01225 446787), a couple of minutes' walk from both stations, will store baggage for around £3 an item. You do not need to be staying in the hostel to use the service.

ENTERTAINMENT

Theatre and cinema

Bath's main venue, the Theatre Royal (tel: 01225 448844, www.theatreroyal.

Above: an old-fashioned post box.

org.uk), runs a varied selection of comedies and dramas (some appearing before their West End bow), musicals, ballet and opera. The smaller Ustinov studio next door has more experimental work while the egg theatre shows productions for children and families.

Housed in a former cinema, Komedia (22–23 Westgate Street; tel: 0845 293 8480; www.komedia.co.uk/bath) is a leading live entertainment venue with a mix of comedy, music and cabaret shows. Every Saturday night, it hosts the popular Krater Comedy Club. It is also home to The Arts Café, serving Fairtrade coffees and teas, and meals using local produce.

There's a multiscreen Odeon cinema (James Street West; tel: 0871 224 4007; www.odeon.co.uk) showing the latest blockbusters. For more arthouse fare and other offerings, try the excellent Little Theatre cinema (St Michaels Place; tel: 0871 902 5735; www.picturehouses.co.uk).

Nightlife

With its large student community, Bath has a lively club and bar scene. Moles (14 George Street) is a Bath institution, having been around since 1978. Among the bands to have played there are Blur, The Cure, Eurythmics, Manic Street Preachers, Massive Attack, Oasis, Pulp, Radiohead, The Smiths, and The Killers. It was voted the country's best venue for upcoming bands in the UK in 2013 (Music Blog Awards). Not bad for a little club. The building also houses a café and a music studio. Po Na Na (8 North Parade), an underground club with a Moroccan interior, is another popular nightclub. The Common Room (2 Saville Row) is a stylish bar for relaxing, drinking cocktails or dancing until late.

Bath also has a fabulous range of pubs. The Star on the Paragon is a classic traditional old boozer; the Old Green Tree at 12 Green Street, with its lovely oak panelling, is another classy pub; the Bell Inn on Walcot Street is a good music venue, popular with Bath's alternative scene; the Coeur de Lion in Northumberland Passage is Bath's smallest pub; the Pig and Fiddle on Saracen Street is popular hangout for students, and rugby fans and football; the Raven on Queen Street does a great pie and a pint; and the White Hart in Widcombe is a winner, especially for its lovely grub.

Gay and lesbian

There is not a prominent gay scene in Bath. Nearby Bristol has one of the largest LGBT communities in the country with a flourishing nightlife, centred on the Old Market Quarter. Worth checking out are the Pineapple pub (37 George Street; www.omg bristol.ning.com). Also popular are Queenshilling (9 Frogmore Street; www.queenshilling.com) and the Old Market Tavern (29–30 Old Market Street; www.omtbristol.com).

Accommodation

The good news is that, being such a popular destination, there is a wide range of tourist accommodation in Bath. The bad news is that Bath hotel prices are among the most expensive in the UK outside London, due to its preponderance of luxury hotels. So booking ahead is essential, especially in summer and on weekends. If you're searching for a bargain, steer clear of the more high-end hotels and look for the cheaper deals that can be found at the city's guesthouses and B&Bs. Bathwick (over Pulteney Bridge), the Upper Bristol Road or the Wells Road are all rich in B&Bs. You may find that at peak season some places want visitors to stay for at least two nights. The price-codes listed in this section are based on a standard double room for one night in peak season. Breakfast included, unless otherwise stated.

£££   over £150
££   £80–150
£   under £80

Above: there are numerous hotels within easy reach of the city centre.

CITY CENTRE

The Halcyon
2–3 South Parade; tel: 01225 444100; www.thehalcyon.com.
This 21-room hotel, in a Georgian town house close to the railway station, offers organic breakfasts (extra charge) and stylish bedrooms with the latest technology. Licensed bar. ££

Harington's
8 Queen Street; tel: 01225 461728; www.haringtonshotel.co.uk.
In a picturesque cobbled street near Queen Square, this charming boutique hotel has 13 tastefully decorated and surprisingly quiet en-suite rooms. Helpful staff. Reserved parking nearby. ££

The Henry
6 Henry Street; tel: 01225 424052; www.thehenry.com.
Decent B&B that scores for its location close to the shops and a short walk from the railway station. Seven rooms, each with TV, Wi-fi, and tea- and coffee-making facilities. Minimum two-night stay at weekends. ££

SACO serviced apartments
31–40 St James's Parade; tel: 01225 486540; www.bath.sacoapartments.com/bath.
If you're looking for something a bit different, try these serviced apartments near the Southgate shopping centre. Handsomely restored, with bright, airy rooms, Italian designer furniture, kitchens with all mod cons and spotless bathrooms. Minimum two-night stay at weekends. ££

Three Abbey Green
3 Abbey Green; tel: 01225 428558; www.threeabbeygreen.com.
B&B in a town house dating from 1689 with seven bright, spacious and individually decorated rooms. The flagship room, the Lord Nelson, has a four-poster bed and a real-flame gas fire.

Stylish, contemporary apartments also available in the same square. ££–£££

YMCA

International House, Broad Street; tel: 01225 325900; www.bathymca.co.uk. Young man, forget all the jokes, this is an excellent budget option. Basic accommodation (dorm rooms, singles and doubles). The YMCA is a not-for profit organisation. £

UPPER TOWN

The Bath Priory

Weston Road; tel: 01225 331922; www.thebathpriory.co.uk.

One of Bath's best luxury hotels. An exquisite Gothic-style country house west of Victoria Park. It has 27 luxuriously appointed rooms, spa and sauna facilities, a swimming pool and a superb Michelin-starred restaurant overseen by chef, Sam Moody. Ask for a room with a balcony overlooking the beautiful gardens. £££

Brocks

32 Brock Street; tel: 01225 338374; www.brocksguesthouse.co.uk.

An elegant Georgian property, between the Circus and the Crescent, with eight light, comfortable rooms. ££

Francis Hotel

Queen Square; tel: 01173 199006; www.mgallery.com.

After a £6 million refurbishment, the Francis has been returned to its former glory and all 98 rooms are furnished to a high standard. You can dine at the ad-joining Brasserie Blanc. ££–£££

Marlborough House

1 Marlborough Lane; tel: 01225 318175; www.marlborough-house.net.

Imposing stone Victorian house with six spacious, tastefully decorated rooms furnished with antiques, flat-screen TVs and free Wi-fi. Minimum two-night stay at weekends. Delicious organic breakfasts, caters to guests with special diets. Genial host. ££

The Queensberry Hotel

Russel Street; tel: 01225 447928; www.thequeensberry.co.uk.

The place to go if you're looking for somewhere stylish, quirky and quintessentially British. Ask for the first-floor bedrooms with their high ceilings and authentic Georgian colours; 29 rooms in all. There are delightful walled gardens and the excellent Olive Tree restaurant. £££

The Royal Crescent Hotel

15–16 The Royal Crescent; tel: 01225 823333; www.royalcrescent.co.uk.

Your chance to stay in Bath's ultimate address, right in the middle of the sweeping crescent. The 45 individually decorated rooms overlook gardens or parkland and the suites are named after local figures, such as Beau Nash and Jane Austen. There's also a posh restaurant and spa. £££

PULTENEY BRIDGE

Apple Tree Guest House

7 Pulteney Gardens, tel: 01225 337642; www.appletreeguesthouse.co.uk.

A recent makeover has made this a charming place to stay and it comes with the bonus of off-street parking. Six beautifully decorated rooms and extensive breakfast menu complete the picture. ££

Bath Youth Hostel

Bathwick Road; tel: 0845 371 9303; www.yha.org.uk.

This Italianate mansion has 121 beds and is about a mile (1.6km) from the city centre, up a hill, but is worth seeking out if you're looking for budget accommodation. You don't have to be a member of the YHA to stay. Licensed café/bar. £

Dukes

Great Pulteney Street; tel: 01225 787960; www.dukesbath.co.uk.

Experience a taste of life in a Georgian town house on one of Bath's grandest streets. Under new ownership in 2012,

Above: first-floor bedroom at The Queensberry Hotel.

all 17 rooms are tastefully appointed with period furniture and fine fabrics. Parking permits provided. ££–£££
Macdonald Bath Spa Hotel
Sydney Road; tel: 0844 879 9106; www.macdonaldhotels.co.uk/bathspa.
One of the city's leading lights, a five-star hotel set in its own extensive grounds near Sydney Gardens. Pamper yourself in its acclaimed health and leisure spa or indulge yourself at one of its two restaurants. There are 129 luxurious bedrooms, with a private butler service available in some suites. More efficient than charming. £££
Villa Magdala
Henrietta Road; tel: 01225 466329; www.villamagdala.co.uk.
With 20 stylish boutique rooms, this luxury B&B is located on a quiet street just a five-minute walk from the city centre. The award-winning breakfast includes complimentary Bucks Fizz and excellent coffee. Parking available. ££–£££
The White Guest House
23 Pulteney Gardens; tel: 01225 426075; www.thewhiteguesthouse.co.uk.
Covered with flowers in season, this five-roomed B&B is a former winner of the Bath in Bloom competition. Well located on a quiet street with free parking. £

RIVER WALK (TOUR 5)
Bath Paradise House Hotel
86–88 Holloway; tel: 01225 317723; www.paradise-house.co.uk.
In the south of the city, and less than 10 minutes from the city centre, this hotel has spectacular views. The rooms have a country-house feel with lovely bathrooms. Three of the 11 rooms have four-poster beds. Look for special deals. ££–£££
Combe Grove Hotel
Brassknocker Hill; tel: 01225 834644; www.pumahotels.co.uk.
This woodland hotel, set in 69 acres (30 hectares), offers glorious views of the valleys around Bath and has 42 rooms. Facilities include a health club and an impressive restaurant. ££–£££
White Hart
Widcombe Hill; tel: 01225 313985; www.whitehartbath.co.uk.
A former coaching inn, this excellent gastro-pub offers some of the best-value accommodation in the city. The four double rooms are close to the pub so it's not ideal if you're planning an early night. Book in advance for its backpacker dorms and family rooms. £

OUTSIDE THE CITY CENTRE
Apsley House Hotel
141 Newbridge Hill; tel: 01225 336 966; www.apsley-house.co.uk.
This elegant Georgian country-house hotel, built in 1830 by the Duke of Wellington, has been refurbished to offer modern comforts. It's furnished with fine antiques and original oil paintings. The 12 rooms are a little on the flouncy side, with four-poster beds in some. A lovely garden and free parking. ££–£££
Athole Guest House
33 Upper Oldfield Park; tel: 01225 320000; www.atholehouse.co.uk.
This award-winning B&B is a chintz-free zone. It's a 15-minute walk from the city centre, but the welcoming

hosts provide free transfers to the bus and railway stations. There are four inviting bedrooms with king-size or twin beds, free Wi-fi and digital TV. ££

Bloomfield House

146 Bloomfield Road; tel: 01225 420105; www.ecobloomfield.com.

B&B in large 19th-century neoclassical house that boasts excellent eco-credentials. Some of the eight rooms have four-poster or half-tester beds. Breakfasts are organic and locally sourced. A longish walk to the centre. ££

Dorian House

1 Upper Oldfield Park; tel: 01225 426336; www.dorianhouse.co.uk.

Classy accommodation in an elegant Victorian town house run by a London Symphony Orchestra cellist. The 12 rooms are named after classical musicians. ££

The Hollies

Hatfield Road; tel: 01225 313366; www.theholliesbath.co.uk.

Reasonably priced accommodation in a grade II listed Victorian property with three individually designed rooms, that's a 15-minute walk from the city centre. Wi-fi available. Lovely garden. No children under 16. £–££

One Three Nine

139 Wells Road; tel: 01225 314769; www.139bath.co.uk.

An excellent, contemporary boutique B&B with 14 gorgeous rooms, which complement the Victorian building. A warm welcome and delicious breakfasts make this the perfect choice. ££–£££

OUTSIDE BATH

Babington House

Babington, near Frome; tel: 01373 812266; www.babingtonhouse.co.uk.

This exclusive venue is located in magnificent parkland, 12 miles (20km) outside Bath. Luxurious and stylish with 32 rooms, it's immensely popular with the London media set. There's a spa, pool, gym, crèche, lakeside walks, and a heli-

Above: Lucknam Park, outside Bath.

copter landing site, should you need one. First-rate service and food. £££

Lucknam Park

Colerne, Wiltshire; tel: 01225 742777; www.lucknampark.co.uk.

Top luxury country house/spa, with 48 rooms, set in 500 acres (200 hectares) of parkland about 6 miles (10km) from Bath. The palatial Palladian mansion has an award-winning restaurant with a Michelin star. Extensive leisure facilities including an equestrian centre. £££

Manor House Hotel

Castle Combe; tel: 01249 782206; www.manorhouse.co.uk.

This 14th-century building is set in more than 300 acres (120 hectares) of wood and parkland with a championship golf course. The Bybrook restaurant offers an impressive menu. £££

WEBSITES

The Tourist Information Centre operates a room booking service for a small fee (tel: 0844 847 5256; www.visitbath.co.uk).

Guesthouses/B&Bs: the Bath Independent Guest Houses Association (www.bigha.co.uk) has listings for over 100 leading B&Bs and guesthouses.

Self-catering: the Landmark Trust (www.landmarktrust.org.uk) is involved in the restoration and letting of historic buildings, including several in Bath.

Index

Credits

Insight Great Breaks Bath
Written by: Piero Bohoslawec, Dorothy
Stannard
Updated by: Jackie Staddon, Hilary Weston
Edited by: Tom Stainer
Art Editor: Tom Smyth
Production: Tynan Dean, Rebeka Davies
Series Editor: Sarah Clark

All Pictures APA/Corrie Wingate except:
Alamy 45B, 97, 114; Bigstock 99; Elliot
Brown 65; Courtesy Bath and North East
Somerset Council 16; Rebecca C 28; Lawrei
Cate 104; Stephen Cole 102B; Corbis 2/3,
6/7; Heather Cowper 31, 52, 84; Thomas
Deucing 85; Dreamstime 83, 95, 98; Fotolia
91; Getty Images 40/41, 71; Uli Harder 36;
Istockphoto 47, 96, 101, 106; APA Lydia Evans
4BL/TL, 5BL/TL, 20T, 23B, 29, 37B, 38T,
61C; Stephen Jones 89; Simon Keeping 100T;
Craig Loftus 30; Fernando Mafra 76/77; Mary
Evans 73, 77M/T; Kunal Mehta 22; Tyo Mitch
44; Courtesy the Natural Theatre Company
66B; Marilyn Peddle 102; The Queesberry
Hotel 125; Rex Features 95T; Karen Roe
74; Andrew Sales 5MR; Stu Smith 111; Hans
Splinter 72; Lauren Tucker 100B; Visit Bath
21B, 24B, 35, 69, 117; Courtesy Warner
Brothers 68; Andrew Wilkinson 5TR, 64T;
Graham Well 14; Ann Wuyts 105
Cover pictures by: APA/Corrie Wingate

CONTACTING THE EDITORS: As every
effort is made to provide accurate information
in this publication, we would appreciate it
if readers would call our attention to any
errors and omissions by contacting:
Apa Publications, PO Box 7910,
London SE1 1WE, England.
E-mail: insight@apaguide.co.uk

Information has been obtained from sources
believed to be reliable, but its accuracy
and completeness, and the opinions based
thereon, are not guaranteed.

© 2014 APA Publications (UK) Ltd.
Second Edition 2014

Printed in China by CTPS

Map Production: Phoenix Mapping and APA
Cartography Department; Mapping contains Meridian 2 data © Crown copyright
and database right and other elements ©
OpenStreetMap and contributors, CC-BY-SA.

Worldwide distribution enquiries:
APA Publications GmbH & Co. Verlag KG
(Singapore Branch), 7030 Ang Mo Kio Ave 5
08-65 Northstar @ AMK, Singapore 569880
apasin@singnet.com.sg
Distributed in the UK and Ireland by:
Dorling Kindersley Ltd
(a Penguin Company)
80 Strand, London, WC2R 0RL, UK
sales@uk.dk.com
Distributed in the United States by:
Ingram Publisher Services
1 Ingram Boulevard, PO Box 3006,
La Vergne, TN 37086-1986
ips@ingramcontent.com